THE BIG LIES & ABSOLUTE TRUTH! MAKING MONEY IN THE GREATEST GOLD RUSH IN HISTORY

Making Money in Precious Metals and Rare Coins: How to Maximize Your Profit

NICK GROVICH

Published by Essential Direct, Phoenix, AZ.

Printed in the United States of America

Cover Design by diMO digital
Scottsdale, AZ

TABLE OF CONTENTS

Dedications

The most important person in my coin career is my dad, Robert Grovich. He introduced me to rare coins. He also made innumerable trips to the bank to get coins for me to look through. Plus, he became my very first investor!

When I graduated from Penn State, it was he who found me my first job at a coin and bullion investment house. Later, he encouraged me when I went on my own.

SECTION I

DON'T MISS OUT ON THE REAL PROFITS

In this section, I want make sure you understand the difference between the appreciation of the gold, silver, and bullion markets as compared with rare coins.

CHAPTER 1
Time for a Change into a Better Investment

If you already own coins, this book is intended to explain how you got where you are and what's really happening in the coin, gold, and silver world.

You likely believed that rare coins would skyrocket right along with the gold, silver, and platinum markets. They did not.

In this updated version of my book, I not only show you what to watch out for but draw on what has happened the last eleven years as gold, silver, and platinum took off. I now have proof of what I wrote in the first book. If you read the book and stayed with rare coins, you are likely disappointed. Even if you purchased gold-related coins like St Gaudens or $20 Liberties, you fell behind.

Factors, including ever-changing markets and increased government regulations, will continue to shape the rare coin market. Many of the touted benefits of rare coins are nonexistent, and most real benefits are shared by lower-risk, more liquid bullion coins such as Eagles and Buffalo Gold coins.

If you truly believe in gold, the failure of the dollar, and more political unrest, it's time to make a change.

If your coins are worth less now than when you bought them, I will explain how that happened, why it happened, why it isn't completely your fault, and what you can do about it. Since my last book, many of the highly promoted coins have actually fallen in value, while gold has continued to hit new highs.

But, if you have not purchased coins or you intend to continue purchasing, I urge you to read this book before you answer any telephone call that might have a marketer/dealer trying to sell you coins.

I'll help you understand how buying, selling, and collecting coins and bullion really works.

I'll give you the hard facts about investing in both the good and the bad. If you have more questions, I'll tell you where you can get the answers.

I don't deal in theory unless I can back it up with fact. Many dealers have not liked what's in this book, because it will expose many of the fallacies they continue to promote. I invited dealers to prove me wrong, but none have.

Why, if I am a coin dealer, do I not promote rare coins? The reason is simple. I used to, and my clients made a lot of money. Some made 300 % or more in just a few years. As time passed, however, it became increasingly hard to make profits. Sure, some of the $20 St Gaudens and Liberties have gone up simply because they have a large amount of gold in them, but in practically every case, they lagged the bullion markets. I simply got tired of telling clients they were losing money. I wanted to find out why they were not getting ahead.

I decided to investigate what the market was doing instead of spouting the theories and myths of rare coins like almost every other dealer. It's hard for a dealer to be honest and unbiased when they have to come up with reasons to sell rare coins. I was taught as an economics student at Penn State University that the main factor in assessing any problem was to not already have your hypothesis. If you have decided the answer, you make the facts fit the outcome you want. I did the research openly and candidly and then reached the conclusions found in this book. Unfortunately, they were not what I or most other dealers would like. Others continue to plain out ignore the facts. They only want to shape the "facts" to their foregone conclusion.

They will pull out charts and graphs and tell you I'm wrong based on the same ill-formed and unproven theories they've relied on for over twenty-five years. What they still can't produce are clients who have benefited from these theories. I find it sadly funny that they point to clients making 10 to 70 % profits on coins like Platinum Eagles, when platinum has gone up more than 500 percent! There are some investors who did okay, but the overwhelming majority, probably 90 % or more, have not! This is based on thirty years of experience.

The purpose of this book is to educate you on the absolute facts of the gold and rare coin business and enable you to make money on your gold, silver, and rare coin investments.

I have owned American Federal Rare Coin and Bullion since 1985 and was employed or worked in the coin and bullion markets since 1980.

My experience included every aspect of the rare coin and bullion market. I went from collector to salesman to marketer. For years, I managed a sales team of brokers. I did telephone sales, spoke at seminars, and was interviewed on the radio. For over twenty-seven years, I was (and to a degree still am) a wholesale buyer and seller, attending major coin shows and auctions across the country.

I have written articles and done taped interviews for Dr. Gary North, author of the *Remnant Review Newsletter, Firestorm Chats, and Investment Coin Review*. I am also proud of being recommended by Robert Prechter in his book, *Conquer the Crash*.

There was even a time I was a licensed commodities broker.

So you see, I've been in every aspect of the coin and bullion market from collector to investor to telemarketer and finally, to wholesale supplier.

I am a member of many notable organizations, as any good dealer should be. Among them are:

- Professional Numismatic Guild (PNG), Member #553
- American Numismatic Association (ANA), Life Member #5211
- Professional Coin Grading Service (PCGS), Member #33
- Numismatic Guaranty Corp (NGC)
- Florida United Numismatics, Life Member #711
- Central States Numismatic Society
- Society of Commemorative Coins
- Texas Numismatic Association

The point I'm making is that I am sharing real-world experiences and stories.

My love of coins got me into this business. However, after becoming a professional dealer, my views changed substantially.

In the 1980s, the coin environment was expanding and booming, and I was successfully selling coins to investors as well as supplying dealers. For the first decade of being a dealer, I believed in the virtues of rare coins. In many cases, I still do, although I'm now more realistic. I was a successful investor for my dad and myself before ever becoming a dealer. I believed a lot of the doomsday scenarios and worked for people who espoused them.

It's easy to get caught up in these scenarios and be blindsided because of tunnel vision.

There were some great opportunities to make money in the first ten years I was a dealer.

However, in the 1990s, prices stagnated and then dropped. The vast majority of investors, as well as dealers, weren't doing well. It was depressing to tell people day after day that they were losing money. Usually, they blamed the dealer for the market's woes. Even the cream of the crop dealers could rarely make money for their clients. Before you knew it, people held coins for years and years, only to watch them lose more and more of their value.

Fifteen years ago, I urged investors to stay out of coins. For the most part, that has been good advice. I recommended buying gold over rarities. That has been and will likely continue to be good advice.

I never thought gold would move as far as it has, but I still knew coins would not match its performance. Time has proven that to be correct.

Many people who have been talked into investing in rare coins are now in their seventies, eighties, and even nineties. As profits disappeared and losses compounded, I had to take a close look at the business and the market. I started to realize several things.

The first thing I noticed that concerned me both in my personal investing and in the marketplace was that many people, including myself, were investing with one thing in mind: disaster. That's right, people were planning only for economic collapse, inflation, political chaos, and so on.

Of course, dealers sold into the paranoia. That's not to say our world doesn't have problems. It does, and we should all be concerned, and having some gold as insurance or even speculation is fine (more about this later). But, there are many people who have a disproportionate amount of money in rare coins—people who honestly know very little about them. On top of that, the rare coins they buy for "protection" most likely will be worthless if their fears are ever realized. It's a no-win situation.

Add to this grim outlook the outrageous markups, the outright created, manipulated markets that are too common throughout the industry, and it becomes obvious that the uninformed investor doesn't stand a chance.

This book has many of my peers despising me, because they consider me bad for the industry. They don't want anyone to tell people to not buy coins or, worse yet, to sell out. Many even take great efforts to keep buyers in the dark. They don't want anyone to explain the inner workings of the market or why, in my opinion, over 90 % of coin buyers lose the bulk of their money. They also don't want people to learn why many dealers are interested in selling coins to everyone they can. They tout the "free market," "supply and demand," and "hedge" aspects of the coin market. If we all just keep selling coins to investors, that will solve the problem, they chant. But it doesn't.

Even worse than selling these coins with wild stories of the riches to be made is the fact that many dealers provide only a one-way market. They'll gladly sell you coins, but they seldom, if ever, will buy those coins back from you. They certainly don't want to share with you how to find the true market value of a coin, even though it is relatively easy to do. You won't find real prices on any Internet sites I've found. In fact, in my opinion, the prices you find are very deceptive and guarantee you will overpay.

Therefore, when investors decide to take a loss or move on, it's very difficult for them. Dealers will stall them, not return their calls, or flat out tell them off when they want to sell. Many will simply trade you into other coins in an effort to hide the true value of your coins.

It is my hope that this book does several things for you:

1. **If you want to invest in bullion or rare coins:** This book will show you how to do it the right way. This includes getting the best price when you buy and having something liquid when you want to sell. If I do nothing more than show you how to save 20 % on your coin purchase, I will have made you money.
2. **If you already have coins:** This book will explain how you got where you are and the real inside market. It will explain the half-truths and outright lies you've been told and show you how to "test" your dealer. Most important, it will give you "hard facts," so you can evaluate whether you really should be in coins. Hopefully, it will convince you to get out

of the rare coin market unless you are a true collector.

3. **It will provide you an honest resource** about the rare coin market—more than just the hype created by dealers to sell you coins.

While brokers do in fact promise you the moon, it's still you, the buyer, who has the responsibility to do the research. In fact, this has been further affirmed by a Supreme Court ruling that basically says it's the buyer's responsibility to determine if commissions, markups, or fees are in line. This ruling will likely bolster dealers' aggressive pricing and misinformation that is disseminated on the Internet

Hopefully, this book will open your eyes and show you the real inside workings of this market.

I do paint a rather bleak picture in many chapters. You should know that as a collector, I love rare coins. If you are willing to put the time and effort into learning the market and working with a reputable dealer (there are many), it can be mentally and financially rewarding. To do this you must learn from others' mistakes.

I was chagrined to learn that my book is openly discussed on a few blogs. I never dreamed it would raise a commotion. I do find it interesting how many buyers are defending dealers. I hope that means they have found the good ones. I'm afraid some still defend rare coins just so they won't be "wrong."

CHAPTER 2
THE MARKET TODAY

If you are a collector, there are many chapters you may be tempted to skip. You have probably learned much of what I'll mention through personal experience. Please don't skip, though, because by reading all of the chapters, you'll either confirm your knowledge or add to it.

I believe the coin market today offers unparalleled opportunities for collectors and even investors who want to take a hands-on approach.

Many of the finest dealers in the country have started to focus on the serious investor or collector. However, many have become dependent on high-pressure salespeople with a, "sell a coin with any scare tactic," mentality. They will outright lie about confiscation and reporting requirements, as well as make up facts about "historic" performance of coins.

I believe this is the beginning of an entirely new type of market. It's refreshing to see dealers offer coins as something besides "get rich quick" investments.

In reality, it's a step backward as much as forward, because it is a return of investors being sold coins that have to almost double in price just to break even. Then, they will find their dealer unwilling to repurchase the coins.

It's an ever-shrinking and manipulated market. Few investors return to buying coins once they figure out how the market really operates.

CHAPTER 3
THE WRONG COINS FOR THE RIGHT REASONS

People have been worried about the safety of their money for decades. Some are worried about the government currency printing presses running nonstop. Others worry about the direction of government policies and actions they see as repressive, confiscating, and morally offensive.

We have all read stories of the German inflation in the 1920s and the exodus of the Jewish people from Europe in the 1930s and 1940s, to name just a few instances when fiat money was of questionable value.

The conflict between gold as "real" money and currency goes back to the mid-1800s in this country and continues today. It is not my intent to examine the arguments for or against gold in this book. I believe most people will have already gained at least some knowledge through historical research, while others may have garnered their information through scary newsletters, apoplectic books, and plain old scare tactics used by those trying to sell coins and bullion.

A rather astute gentleman I recently dealt with had approximately $90,000 worth of gold stored in an Austrian bank. Unfortunately, the bank decided to discontinue its storage program and ended up transferring his gold to him here in the United States.

He was unsure what to do with the gold, so he called dealers for help. He contacted one dealer who convinced him that he should buy so-called rare date Platinum Eagles and $20 Liberty coins, as they would protect him better.

By the time the trade was done and a couple years had passed, he had lost over $46,000 of the value of his investment, all while he was supposedly buying safe coins. To add further insult, gold had gone up over almost 20 % during the same period. Years later, gold jumped again, nearly doubling, while his rare gold coins went up only a fraction of that. He lost well into the hundreds of thousands. After platinum tripled, he finally broke even on his graded Eagles.

Be careful that when you are buying gold to protect and hedge yourself that you are really getting what you think you are. You should be after bullion coins, such as Gold Eagles, Krugerrands, Maple Leafs, or other coins that trade daily with the price of gold, with only a small charge over the spot price.

Unfortunately, many of the rarer coins will not move with the price of gold. My research has shown that the vast majority of numismatic gold coins have gone up much less than half as much as gold. Gold has gone up in multiples since 1999. In many cases, so-called semi-numismatics have barely broken even.

Don't complicate gold by buying rare coins or numismatics that will reduce your liquidity and profits. Buy only bullion-related coins.

Gold certainly may have a place in your portfolio if it addresses your personal concerns, but be sure you know what you are buying. Unfortunately, there are many companies that advertise on TV and radio, among other places, and talk about the roaring bull market in gold. They get big-name sponsors to confirm that gold is the only way to protect your assets.

When you call to purchase the gold, the broker will try his or her best to sell you some type of rare or semi-rare coin. They will give you every reason in the world why gold bullion coins are not what you want. Instead, they will claim that 20 Francs, $20 St Gaudens or Liberties, Proof Eagles or certified Eagles are what you need. It's called bait and switch.

Stick with what you want to buy. Most likely, that is simply gold bullion coins like U.S. gold Eagles or Buffaloes, Krugerrands, Maple Leaf coins, or Philharmonics.

The salespeople may scare you with false claims that the coins they are offering are not subject to confiscation or reporting.

Many dealers simply don't like to sell gold bullion or bullion-type coins because the markup is so small. Instead, they will try and talk you, the buyer, into a variety of gold type coins with a commission that can be as much as 100 % higher!

client of mine in Texas called me to report that he took my advice way back in 1999 and sold his portfolio of $2 ½ Indians and $20 Liberties for a little more than half of what he paid: $180,000. It was a loss of over $120,000. He put the money into gold Eagles, and today his coins are worth over $720,000. Had he kept his original rare coin portfolio, he would be worth only about $225,000.

He took a loss when he realized he had been sold the wrong coins and turned that loss into a great investment.

Sometimes, the hardest thing to do is to realize that you were sold the wrong coins and take the first step in the right direction to maximize profits.

It's your responsibility as a buyer to make sure that you buy the coin that best fits your circumstance: make sure that you buy the right coin, at the right price, at the right time. Too often, a broker may push the promoted item of the day instead of listening to your needs.

Ask yourself if what's being offered is what you want. I've seen many "investors" who have paid in excess of $3,700 per ounce for platinum coins, while platinum was selling for less than half of that amount. The same scenario holds true for gold and so-called "rare" modern gold coins, from rare date or graded Eagles to a variety of foreign gold coins.

CHAPTER 4
HEDGING VERSUS SPECULATING

Gold may be a great hedge, or it can be the worst investment you ever buy.

If you are interested in a hedge (not an investment) and sleep better having a little gold and silver under the bed, stick with gold and silver bullion coins (see chapter 33).

Hedging is still okay if you understand what a hedge really is. A hedge is any investment that cushions a portion of your other investments if they turn south. A hedge is not putting all your money in any area or investment because you're convinced a major event will occur.

Some people had all their money in stocks in the 1990s because they were sure the market was taking off. A prudent hedge would have included a portion of that in negatively correlated funds. These would have gone up when the market went down. Bear funds would have been another good hedge, again, going up as the stock market goes down.

Unfortunately, most people don't understand hedging and use the term improperly. I meet many people who have large portions of their assets in gold and/or rare coins because they say it's a hedge against inflation or the dollar or a myriad of other concerns. This is true to a degree, but it should be used as a hedge to counter other investments. Otherwise, if they are wrong about inflation, the dollar, and so on, they will only lose. This is what happened to those who "hedged" throughout the 1980s and 1990s. A one-sided hedge is a gamble not a hedge.

I'm not telling you to stay out of gold. I'm simply telling you to understand why you're buying it. You could make money in gold if you get lucky and your timing is right, but that goes for any commodity, from sugar to oil. Don't buy just to get lucky.

At the time of this writing, gold is only about half of what it should be, adjusted for inflation. It's several times the price at its low but still not as high as it ought to be.

There are two ways to interpret that.

1) Gold does not, in fact, keep up with inflation

OR

2) It still can double just to be where it belongs.

Unfortunately, I don't have the correct answer for you.

Gold certainly has its ups and downs, and I believe it is a prudent thing to add to most portfolios. How much to own depends on your personal fears or goals. I do believe it is a much safer, lower-risk investment or hedge than rare coins. It also provides liquidity that no rare or semi-numismatic coin can offer, yet with all the benefits of rare coins.

I will talk much more about gold throughout the book.

Although I am a coin dealer, all the research I did over the past fifteen years has clearly shown that gold bullion–related items are a much better place to put your money.

CHAPTER 5
MARKET TIMING

As with virtually everything, timing is a critical component when adding to any investment portfolio, and rare coins and gold are certainly no exception.

Don't just blindly buy gold because a broker calls you and talks you into it (especially if he's selling rare coins), because it is not always possible to buy at the low or sell at the high. However, a little research could help you enormously.

Don't get excited by TV or radio ads and panic buy. Again, be aware that many of these dealers will advertise gold but switch you to rare coins.

I personally found most advisers or salespeople have been bullish forever, so when gold has made gains, they all yell that they were right. I've seen newsletter writers who were wrong for twenty-three years all of a sudden say, "I told you so," when gold went up.

One person I personally recommend is Robert Prechter, author of the recently revised *Conquer the Crash*, as well as the newsletter the *Elliott Wave Theorist*, and numerous other books (see Recommended Reading in back of this book).

I met with Mr. Prechter in the summer of 2001. This was just before he released his book, *Conquer the Crash*. Although he had been bearish for years, he was expecting a good upward move.

This was at a time most people were bearish on gold, including yours truly. As we know, gold rallied to over $450 by the end of 2004. It then moved to over $1,250 in 2010.

The point is, instead of just believing the eternally optimistic bulls and salespeople, do a little research before buying.

Don't just find articles that tell you what you want to hear. One client told me that the biggest problem I have is that I won't tell people what they want to hear, so they just call dealers who will. Look at information objectively, and if you are buying a sizable amount of gold, subscribe to the *Elliott Wave Theorist* to get a more unbiased view of the market.

Keep in mind that no one will be able to time the market accurately every time, but if you can avoid buying into the mania created at the highs, you can save a lot of money. The more you save, the more gold you can buy at lower prices; thus, the better your hedge.

SECTION II
BULLION CAN MAKE A DRAMATIC DIFFERENCE

The Difference Between Bullion and Rare Coins Can Be Dramatic

CHAPTER 6
YOUR COINS MOVE WITH GOLD, DON'T THEY?

Morgan dollars went up less than one cent for every dollar silver went up, and they were the best performing coin sector since 1990!

It amazes me when I hear dealers claim that rare coins, specifically U.S. gold coins, outperform gold.

One broker actually told a client that for every dollar gold goes up, St. Gaudens MS-63 go up $2 or $3.

There is no formula that will tell you how any rare coin performs in relationship to gold or silver. That's one of the problems. Too many people assume that their coins go up in step with gold or silver. They don't. In fact, that has led to the undoing of many investors. They watch the bullion markets and assume their rare or semi-numismatic coins have appreciated right along with it.

Unfortunately, unless you are diligent and watch prices in *Coin Dealer Newsletter*, you are totally dependant on your dealer to watch your coins for you.

This is one of the most dangerous mistakes you can make. Many of the large retail dealers, the guys who call you on the phone to force-feed you rare coins, have no intention of buying back your coins.

It's almost funny, but almost all of them will tell you to call them first when you decide to sell. They implore you to sell only to them, but when you try to, they won't put the offer in writing, won't fax it to you, and can take days, weeks, or months to give you any indication of price. All because they really don't want you to sell your coins. When you do, it will become too clear how much you overpaid and they under delivered. But they want one more shot at you! They want to trade you into different coins. That way, their profit gets lost in the trade, and you financially get further and further behind.

So, how much do coins go up when gold does? The answer will surprise you.

Of course, the time period chosen has a lot to do with the outcome. Certainly, we could find a time, whether it's a few months or a very specific instance where a $20 gold has gone up $2 for every $1 in gold, but if you are told this is the norm, the way things usually are or a historical ratio, you are being told a lie. This broker either has no clue how coins have performed, or he has not taken the time to see how they have done, even though every coin dealer out there (investors too) can easily find the numbers.

It would inconvenient for him to find out he's wrong.

Is this the person you want advising you? Do you want someone who is either too lazy to check what he is saying or outright lying to make a commission guiding you?

Here are the real answers to the question. I have chosen to use 1999 as my starting point, simply because that is when we started the upward move in gold, silver, and platinum. Believe it or not, it gets worse if you go back to 1990. Since 1990, silver Morgan dollars have gone up less than one cent for every dollar silver has gone up, and they performed the best since 1999 in all areas of the coin market!

- $20 St. Gaudens MS-63 increased about fifty cents for every dollar gold increased.
- Morgan dollars have increased about one cent for every one-dollar increase in silver since 1990.
- $20 Liberty MS-63 (one of the best performing semi-numismatic coins) increased sixty-seven cents for every dollar gold went up.

- $2½ Indians in MS-63 and MS-65 increased about eight cents for every dollar gold increased. (MS-64s increased only thirteen cents).
- Type II $20 Liberty coins increased a paltry two cents for every dollar gold increased.

On average, rare coins increased 27 % since 1999, while gold soared almost 300 %! So, for every dollar gold increased, rare coins went up a miserly nine cents!

I have assembled close to one thousand charts comparing various rare and semi-numismatic coins to gold. It was rare that any of the coins did as well as gold. Keep in mind, when I talk about gold, I include Gold Eagles, Buffaloes, Krugerrands, and so on, not simply gold bars.

A lot of people are under the assumption that when I talk about buying gold, I mean bars. What I mean is any bullion coin that goes up or down daily with the price of gold. The other thing I want to make clear is that gold bars are serial numbered and rarely if ever need to be assayed. Many brokers use this as a ploy to lead you away from gold. In thirty years of business, I have never had to have a name-brand bar assayed.

If you would like to find out how your coins have performed in relation to gold or silver, call 1-800-221-7694, and ask for a performance review.

CHAPTER 7
DON'T REPEAT THE MISTAKES OF THE LAST TEN YEARS WITH RARE COINS

Since the 1989 market crash, most rare or semi-numismatic coins are still in a losing position.

The best sector of the market, as broken out by *Coin Dealer Newsletter*, is up only 11 % since 1990.

To check this fact, I have charted over a thousand different coins in a variety of grades and have found that almost none have come close to keeping up with gold.

Some coins have actually fallen in price as gold has taken off. For example, \$2½ Indian Head gold coins have dropped 58 % at the same time gold doubled.

The bull market in gold started in 1999.

Over the past thirty-five years, many investors have been swayed or motivated by much supposedly authoritative research, charts, analysis, and data that have been offered as "proof positive" that rare coins have outperformed most, if not every, other investment form out there.

Salomon Brothers published investment reports in the 1980s that usually showed coins as a top performer. The standard wisdom was that you bought rare coins for three to five years and could expect somewhere between 15 % and 20 % appreciation a year. Few realized these gains, and in the end, the whole report was scrapped.

PCGS has a number of charts available that show how coins have done. If you take the time to look at the percentage moves, you will see I am correct. A chart can *look* good if one simply adjusts the scale. A \$100 move on a \$2,000 coin can look dramatic if the chart shows only part of the story.

Another dealer claimed that the coins they had been recommending for years were up over 44 %. But, of the hundreds of their clients I have consulted with, no one ever actually made a profit. In fact, I ended up purchasing a collection from one of their clients for just over $700,000, after they refused to give him an offer. He had spent in excess of $1.5 million for these coins.

Probably the worst case I've heard of was a broker claiming that certain coins he sold had appreciated 1,200 % in a single year! I have purchased millions of dollars worth of coins sold by this dealer at an average market value of 50 to 60 % less than what they were sold for. Was there ever a coin or coins that went up 1,200 %? Maybe there were a few, but it was not representative of what this dealer was actually selling to clients.

Other dealers have reams of misinformation purporting to claim that coins have outperformed stocks, CDs, real estate, and almost any other logical investment that can compete for your money.

Look on the Internet, and you will find all sorts of charts that make coins look great. But look at the assumptions they make, and you will find the charts really are not a straight upward line.

Want to find out how your coins have done in comparison to gold, silver, or even another coin? I can print out a comparison chart from the thousand or so I have developed. I used unbiased pricing from *Certified Coin Dealer Newsletter* and *Coin Dealer Newsletter*, just so no one can say I manipulated the facts.

I'm sure if you are like me, you get reams of mail touting the outrageous profit potential of all types of profitable investments, including rare coins. If you've ever responded and bought these "wonder deals," it is likely you've experienced exactly the scenario I'm talking about.

However, certain investors do make money in rare coins

because they either have a true understanding of the market, or they work with one of the dealers who actually monitor their coins and advise people to sell once in a while. You will read about these positive experiences later in the book. Unfortunately, even these people rarely do as well as simply buying bullion coins like Gold Eagles. The sad part is they have much more risk, time, and effort invested to make a smaller return.

It's a fact that, in my nearly thirty years of evaluating thousands of coin portfolios, most coin investors lose money!

How can that be, when the data out there tells you coins do nothing but go up? In fact, the majority of graphs and charts are not false. If you check the sources, the numbers will prove true enough. You can compare prices from the 1940s, 1950s, 1960s, and 1970s to today's prices and see how good they look. In fact, when checking on many of the best-known classic rarities, they are correct!

So, why do most people lose money?

There are several reasons:

Statistics can be manipulated to show anything you want. It's simply a matter of carefully choosing which coins to report on and finding a period that shows what you want. You can pick very specific times and find almost any result you want. This is why I show my charts on a variety of periods, from one year to ten years and beyond.

I try to look at long periods, not just snippets. I generally use 1990 and 1999 as starting points. The reasons are simply that in 1990 (after the coin market had already taken the biggest fall in history), Coin Dealer Newsletter started a Coin Market Index. The reason I also use 1999 as a starting point is that most people would agree this is when the current bull market actually started.

Almost no one uses the Coin Market Index produced by the

Coin Dealer Newsletter. Even though this is the most used and respected source of pricing in the country, evidenced by the almost universal use by dealers, little is ever said about its unbiased reporting.

The index was started in 1990 and tracks most of the major coin issues.

Since 1990, the best performing area of the market is up only 11 %! This means that for every dollar silver went up, the best performing sector in rare coins went up about four cents!

Yes, 11 % in over twenty years. Is that really a market you want to be in? The overall index still has not broken even. Some areas are only worth about 60 % of what they were in 1990.

This leads us to the second reason why the data can look so good.

Most charts, graphs, or comparison data do not take into account markups, spreads, or commissions!

Most dealers will tell you how much coins have appreciated based solely on wholesale prices, which are prices unavailable to the average investor. In fact, they are prices the average investor probably can't even net when they sell.

Here's an example. If a coin has gone from $500 to $750, giving you a 50 % gain, how much would you actually make?

If you pay a common dealer markup of 35 %, you would have actually paid $675 for the "$500" coin. If you buy from some of the big marketers, you may pay 50 % to 100 % more than listed prices, making it even harder to make money. If you sold it back and paid no commission to resell the coin, you would net $75 before shipping expenses of at least another $25. Best-case scenario: you would've netted 15 % on this substantial market move.

If you paid a higher markup (some dealers mark up as much as 100 %) or were forced to pay a commission on the sale, which is likely because dealers are in business to make money, your results would be much worse. Keep in mind, if you buy from some of the big marketers, you may pay 50 % to 100 % more than listed prices, making it even harder to make money. You would likely lose money or be lucky to break even on a 50 % move in the market!

Most coin buyers need a 50 % move just to break even.

GRADING STANDARDS HAVE CHANGED

If we go back in time and look at some of the prices dealers tend to use when assembling graphs or statistics before 1986, the results can be very misleading. We had substantial grading changes in the 1980s, especially in 1986, when the two premier certification services, NGC and PCGS, started.

To compare an MS-65 from 1975, 1979, or even 1982 to an MS-65 graded after 1986 is like comparing apples to oranges. As a general rule of thumb, the average coin grade prior to 1986 will be two or more grades lower by today's standards. Therefore, an MS-65 in 1975 would likely be an MS-63 or lower today.

Using this fact, the appreciation on many coins becomes questionable.

Lately, I have noticed a few dealers posting charts on the Internet that show how prices have appreciated since 1970. These are totally misleading, in my opinion.

Many will point to even the common Morgan dollar, which is worth about $110 in 2010 in MS-65 condition. In the 1970s, they were available for $10 to $12. So, it appears they have done quite well.

However, it is likely that a coin bought as MS-65 in the 1970s would be an MS-63 by today's standards—if you were lucky. This coin would be worth about $35. The problem gets even worse as you compare higher quality and rarer date coins, because a one-grade difference can mean thousands or even tens of thousands of dollars. Based on the *Coin Dealer Newsletter Index*, Morgan dollars are up only 11 % in the past twenty years.

Well-intended economists and financial analysts who are not involved in the market don't have the market understanding to factor this into their data. One well-known "expert" actually states on his Web site that Eagles are *not* legal tender and therefore confiscatable. Not only are they legal tender (they are a $50 gold piece), they are specifically defined as numismatic in the legislation that created them. That should make them much safer from confiscation than that $20 gold pieces this guy sells. People in the coin market have chosen not to check their facts too carefully, because it makes the case for rare coins so much less exciting.

The bottom line is that you absolutely cannot compare rare coin performance the same way you would compare stocks unless you use pricing information on certified PCGS or NGC from 1986 onward.

Does this mean there are no coins that appreciate? There are times when I see quality coins purchased by true collectors thirty-five, forty, and fifty years ago that have appreciated spectacularly. I often buy these from older collectors or their heirs. Even after forty years, real quality still shines through, and some of these coins bring in fantastic money. But this is not the norm; it is a small percentage of collectors or pedigreed coins. These are the coins you read about breaking price records at auctions. They are not what you are likely to buy on the phone from a broker. Some brokers do specialize in these types of super rare coins, but in general, you pay so much for them that you probably won't make money.

I noticed that rare, truly collectible coins have done the best in most cases. Some of the best performers have been the extreme rarities, like the 1913 Liberty nickel, which is now worth over four million dollars! But even this coin has performed worse than gold. The biggest problem with one-of-a-kind or super rarities is you will never be offered these coins at a reasonable price.

I had a client dying to buy a rare Buffalo nickel from a dealer. He swore it had outperformed the market and was so special it would continue to achieve that rate. He is probably right. But the dealer was asking around $75,000 for a coin that listed for about half that amount. So, it *had* to perform better just to break even.

These are rarely the coins sold to novice investors at reasonable prices.

If you overpay for the "right" coin, the overpayment eats up your profit.

The charts, graphs, and supporting data that paint rare coins as a great investment make it seem too black and white, and it's not that simple.

CHAPTER 8
WHY PEOPLE LOSE MONEY IN RARE COINS

I used to think that 90 % of coin investors lose money, but recently realized that it's likely much worse. Unfortunately, learning that 90 % of other coin investors are in the same boat as you is a small consolation.

There are many reasons people lose money when they invest in coins. Most don't realize it's not just the market that causes people to take significant losses. Many dealers will deny this and tell you that the coin market is very profitable. They quote percentages and charts and graphs. What I look at are actual true-life examples. I visit with literally thousands of people every year and have done so since the 1980s. It's interesting that coins look so good on paper but to find someone who actually made money in coins is a rarity. I submit that through my visits with coin investors, 90 % or more of all coin investors lose money, and I challenge anyone to prove me wrong. I'm going to explain why this happens and, if you are holding coins at a loss, what you can do about it.

There are six basic reasons that the majority loses money in rare coins.

Spreads or Markups Are Huge

The actual markups and spreads between what you pay an average broker/dealer and what the true liquidation price is can average well over 35 % to 50 %. Markups are often as high as 100 %. That means you can, and usually do, pay $750 to over $1,000 for a coin that wholesales for only $500. Ask yourself this: Would you buy stocks, real estate, CDs, or any other "investment" if its value had to double for you to break even? I doubt it.

So, why do so many coin buyers do it? I believe the main reason is that they are unaware they're paying such a high price. Many dealers will tell you I'm off my rocker, and they'll make you all kinds of promises and guarantees—verbally. It is imperative that you try to get those promises in writing. Most dealers will not give you any information in writing about actual markups or spreads. It's normal. After all, dealers do have trade secrets to protect, and they are entitled to a profit. But you as an investor also have a right to know what you're getting.

If you're being told a coin is a great deal for $1,000 and you're only being charged a 10 to 15 % markup, it's your responsibility to check the truth of this claim. (I'll explain more about this later in this book. But for now, suffice it to say, two or three phone calls to other dealers will quickly tell you if you're in the ballpark.)

For the record, dealers who are marking up coins 30 to 50 % are not necessarily crooks. They have a legitimate cost of doing business, and that's what it sometimes takes to net a reasonable profit. The problem is, you must decide if it's more than you're willing to pay for a hedge and/or investment.

If you start off paying a 10 to 20 % markup, you may have a good buy and a decent chance of making money. But, if you've paid a markup of 50 % or more, it's going to be hard to overcome. Paying too much up front will destroy your chance of making money or breaking even, no matter how good or rare the coin.

Unless you are very active and go to coin shows, understand the market, and really spend a lot of time researching, don't expect your salesperson to get you the best price. Many are paid based on how high of a mark-up they can get.

Buying the Wrong Coins Because the Spread Is Low

I call this "buying the wrong coin for the right price." I consistently find people who think they are buying great deals on e-Bay or at various auctions. In some cases, you are, in fact, able to buy at true wholesale prices, bringing your spread to very near zero.

The problem here is you often end up with a problem coin: a low-grade coin or something so common dealers have trouble getting rid of them. Remember, if the market is having trouble absorbing the supply of coins being offered, the next and inevitable move is for the price to drop. It's the simple supply-demand equation at work.

I met a preacher in Georgia on one of my many trips. At first, he was hesitant to tell me what he had bought and how much he paid. He did tell me he had approximately three hundred coins, and all were graded by PCGS or NCG, which are the major coin certification companies.

When I visited him in Georgia, he showed me all of his coins. There were boxes and boxes of common coins, like Morgan Silver dollars in MS-64, MS-65, and MS-66; $20 St. Gaudens in MS-61 to MS-66; and $20 Liberty coins in AU-53 to MS-63. Out of three hundred coins, only seven were rare, in my opinion. He had done his homework before I arrived, so he had an idea of the loss he faced.

After we went over his options, he decided he should keep the seven rare coins and sell the balance. Unfortunately, he lost more than 80 % of what he had invested, which was approximately $176,000. He laughed so he wouldn't cry, as he told me he spent $334,300 for coins he was now selling for less than $59,000!

Then he said, "Well, at least I only paid a 2 % commission when I bought."

He would have been better off paying more commission and buying the right types of coins. He also needed a dealer who would have guided him and told him when it was time to consider selling or cutting his losses.

Again, if you're willing to spend a substantial amount of time researching the market, you may, indeed, find true bargains. That doesn't mean just reading all the dealer promos and promises in the various "newsletters" or junk mail. There are a lot of dealers out there competing against you for really good buys, so don't expect one too often.

Perhaps at this point I should remind you there is one market where the spreads are low—by rare coin standards. That's the bullion market for gold, silver, and platinum. Typically, prices are marked up between 3 and 10 %. Plus, it's an easy investment to follow. Please see chapter 33 for specifics.

Market Timing

Timing is everything, as in any other market. You can get the best price in the world at the top of a market and still take heavy losses. Incidentally, I notice that prices are often best, in terms of actual markups over bid, right after a market top. It's easy to buy close to, or even below, wholesale. Dealers or savvy investors often realize the market is heading down, and inventories are almost always very high at these times. This is why prices can tumble literally 30 % or more overnight. I've seen it happen at a single show, during one day of trading! So, in this situation, you pay "the right price" based strictly on the wholesale price at the moment but still take a beating.

The second part of the equation of timing comes down to this simple fact: the only reason for a runaway or bull market is because the majority of people are buying. This sounds obvious, but few people give it a second thought. I hear thousands of people say, "I bought at the peak of market."

The reality is that the two go hand in hand. After all, it wouldn't be a peak unless a huge number of people were buying (demand). That's why most people own not only gold and silver coins but also stocks and real estate at the peak. It's the basis for the whole theory of contrarian investing. If everyone were not blindly buying, there would not be a peak.

Most People Never Sell

If you rely on a dealer to tell you when to get out, you may wait forever. It's not that dealers are necessarily crooked, dumb, or insensitive to your needs; they are just human. They get caught up in the market just like anyone else. How many stockbrokers or analysts told people to sell stocks in 1999, 2000, or even 2001? Did yours? Probably not.

Very few educated dealers got clients out of their coins at profits, even in the roaring bull markets of 1979, 1986, and 1989.

There are several reasons for this. First being very few really thought the market was coming down. When it started to drop, many believed it was just a dip. Sound familiar? Also, because of the weakness in price, they knew they would have trouble unloading your coins into the market, so they didn't tell you to sell.

If some of the largest dealers issued sell signals, they could collapse areas of the market overnight. This is especially true of thinly traded items. As a handful of dealers are promoting an area of the market, they become the support and outlet for the rest of the dealers.

If these same dealers suddenly decide either to stop buying this area of the market, or worse, start selling back into the market, they soon find a void of buyers. They were the buyers; there is no one else to buy if they become sellers. So, even if they wanted to get you out, they can't.

This is a problem I've seen time after time in the coin market, and it creates a one-way market. Dealers talk about "rare" coins as investments, but many sell to unsuspecting investors, as if they are the collector who will never be looking to unload. That's why many coin investments turn into "family heirlooms." It's rarely planned this way. It's simply a result of the way many coins are marketed. This is one reason I suggest that you should have time limits or goals for profit/loss points to sell.

You need to have a say when it's time to sell.

CAUTION

Having a dealer continue to trade you into other coins does not constitute selling. Often, it's a way of making yet another large profit or commission and putting you even further behind in your investment.

Many People Lose Interest After a Few Years of Owning Coins

Frustration is a major contributor to coin losses. After you stop buying coins, you often lose the little contact you had with the market and your dealer.

Most people have a tendency to put the coins in a safe-deposit box and forget them. Not knowing what to do with the coins, or how to do it, simply relegates the coins to oblivion. People hope and pray that if they just put them away, somehow they will miraculously become valuable at some unknown time in the future. On top of that, they hope by some miracle that if this happens, they will somehow be privy to the information and know how to sell the coins. It's just like the old saying, "Why do today what you can put off till tomorrow!"

Lose Touch with the Market

Many people buy bullion or rare coins because of specific worries or concerns such as, Y2K, war, inflation, and collapse of the dollar. As time goes on, many buyers lose touch with their original objective.

I have found that long-term investment usually is another way of saying the investment didn't work out short term. Once you've lost touch, it's probably a sign that you need to get out of the market and funnel your money and efforts somewhere where your interests may lay.

CHAPTER 9
RARE COINS VERSUS BULLION COINS

Dealers often tout U.S. gold, especially $20 Liberties and St. Gaudens, as the best of bullion and the best of rare coins all wrapped up in one.

On the surface, it really does seem to make sense to get the best of both rarity and bullion. The problem is that the theory simply doesn't hold true.

In most cases, gold bullion has done better than semi-numismatic coins, especially when comparing the amount of markup you need just to break even.

In fact, since the lows of 1999, gold has gone up about 300 %. The rare coin market as a whole has only grown 29 %!

Let's look at a variety of coins that are offered to investors as the best way to buy gold. It will be obvious that dealers as a whole have an agenda to maximize profit at the expense of selling you underperforming coins.

I have spent most of a year documenting prices and charting over one thousand different coins in relation to both gold and silver. It was rare to find any coin that outperformed gold or even did as well as gold.

On the following pages, I have included a small sample of the over one thousand graphs I have charted comparing coins to gold. It is important to understand a few things:

- Whenever I talk about gold, I include gold bullion coins such as Gold Eagles and Buffaloes, Krugerrands, Maple Leaves, and any other coins sold as "bullion." Bullion does not mean bars.
- The prices used are based on *Coin Dealer Newsletter* and *Certified Coin Dealer Newsletter*, because these are the most accurate and unbiased prices in the industry. Unlike PCGS

or Trends, these prices show what coins are really selling for between knowledgeable individuals, not the inflated retail prices that provide fat markups to dealers. If you use these other pricing sources, you are, in my opinion, overpaying for your coins.

- The prices used do not include markups. So, the charts are actually weighted heavily in favor of rare coins, and they still far underperformed the bullion markets.
- I have shown performance by looking at one-year, five-year, ten-years and post-1999 (when the current bull market started) time frames. This should make it a fair representation of the market and keeps me from showing snippets of time just to prove my point.

Unfortunately, most dealers and/or brokers look at what their commission is instead of what's good for the buyer.

To summarize some of the results since 1999, the following graphs and facts make it clear that rare coins do not perform like gold.

Pre-1933 U.S. gold coins have gone up only 37 %, while gold increased 290 %

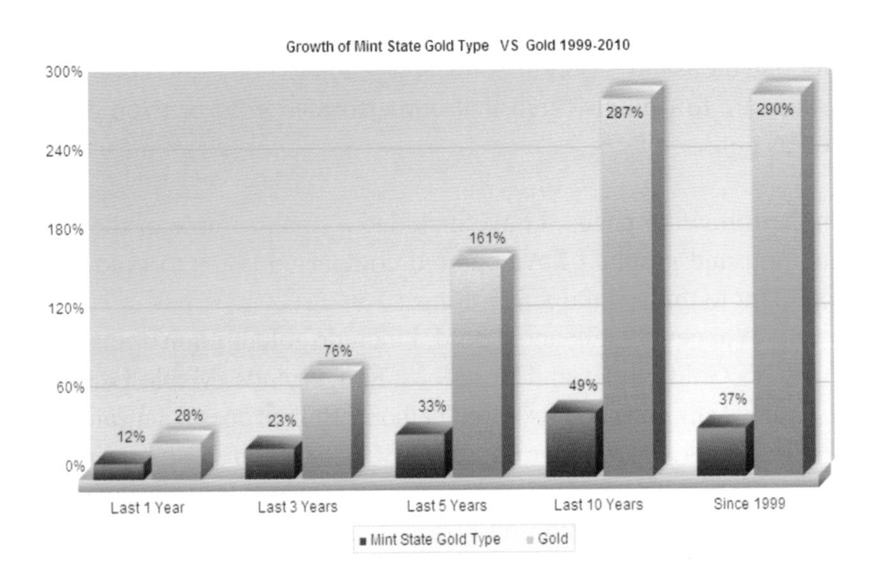

$20 Liberty MS-62 up 6 %, while gold went up 290 %

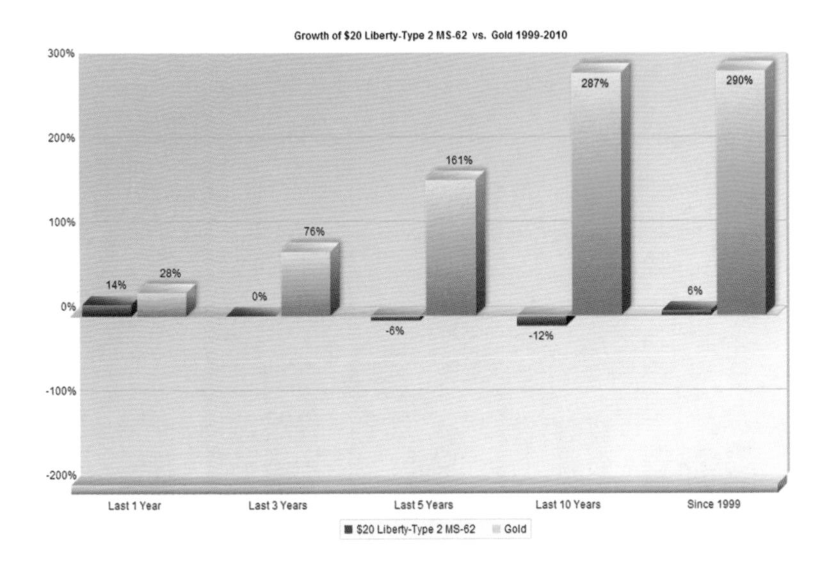

$20 St Gaudens MS-65 up only 124 %, while gold up 290 %

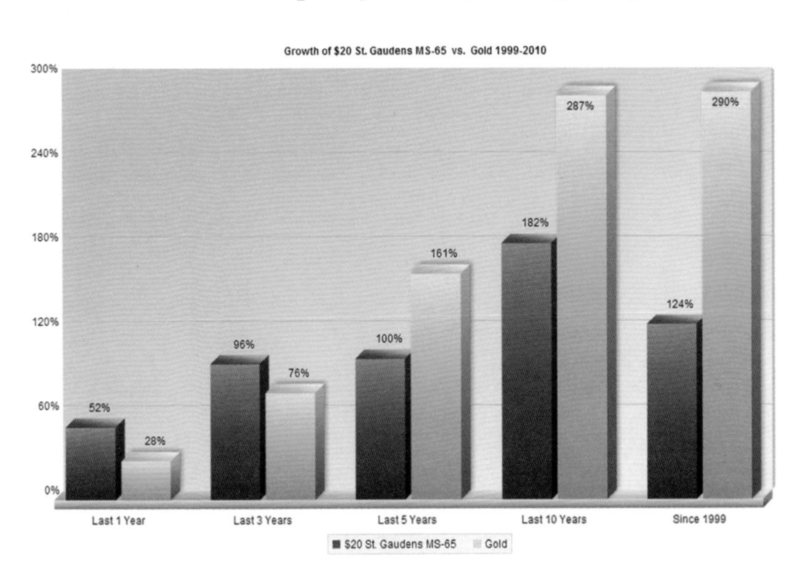

$20 St Gaudens MS-66 up 57 %, with gold up 290 %

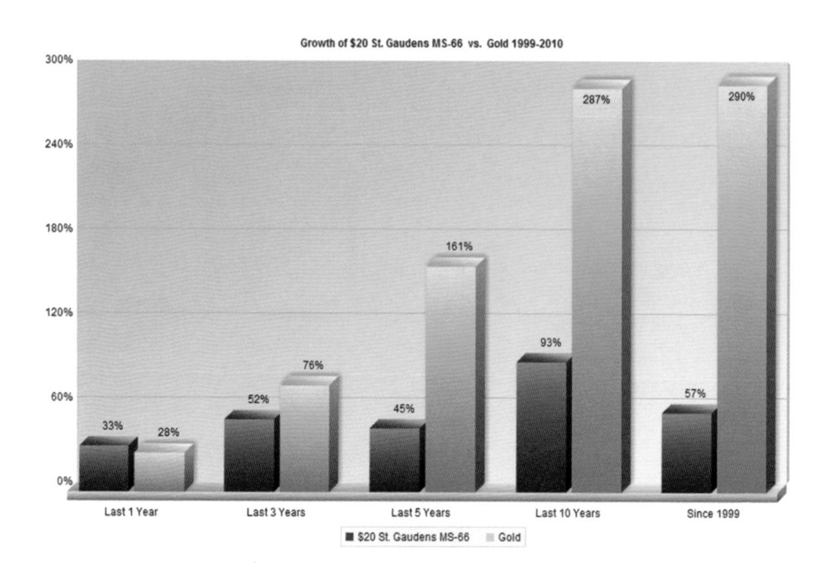

Morgan dollars have gone up only 34 %, while silver is up 256%

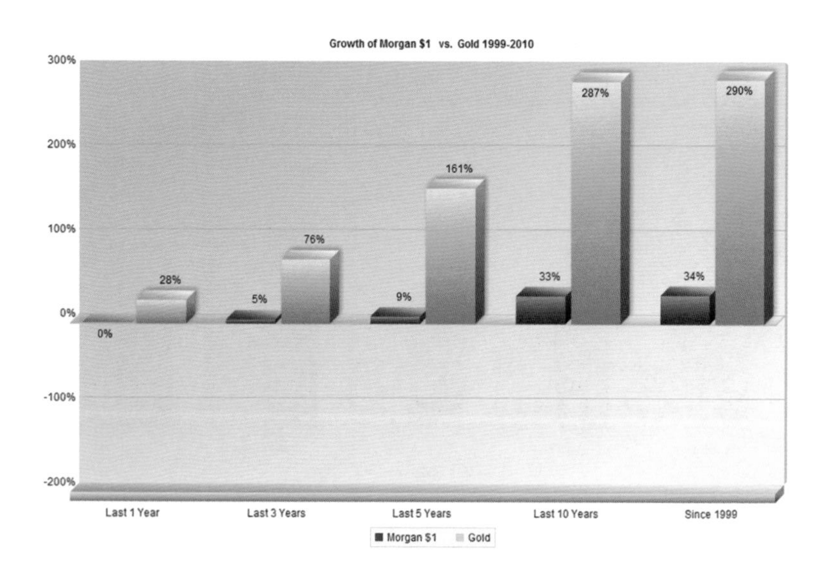

Even the very rare 1911-D $2½ Indian sorely lags gold, with an 86 % jump vs. 290 % for gold!

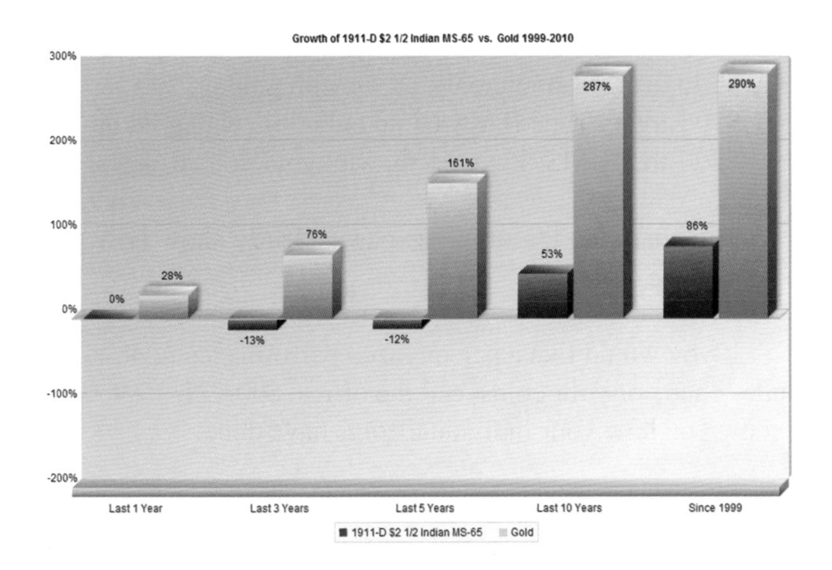

High-powered Proof gold lags, with a 36 % gain against 290 % for gold

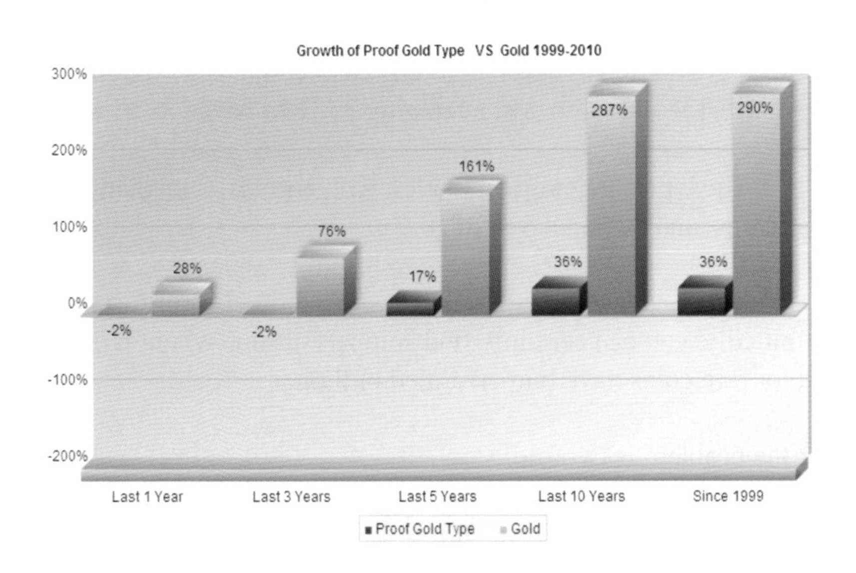

- $2½ Indians in MS-63 went up only 24 %, while gold is up 290 %
- $2½ Indians MS-65 only up 28%, with gold up 290 %
- $3 Gold MS-63 down 10 %, while gold went up 290 %
- $5 Indian MS-65 up only 18 %, with gold up 290 %
- $20 Liberty Type II MS-63 up only 6 %, with gold up 290 %
- $20 Liberty MS-65 up 61 %, with gold up 290 %

The charts on the previous pages clearly show how poorly rare coins have done.

If you would like a personalized performance review, which includes charts of your coins, call the office, 800-221-7694, and we can show you how your individual coins have done.

If you are in the rare coin market, this should provide all the evidence you need to convince you to trade into gold coins like Gold Eagles or Buffaloes. Rare coins simply do not move with the price of gold or silver. Dealers will argue and claim I am wrong. Ask them for proof. Why do they insist on making false claims?

Typical markups on $20s and other U.S. gold range from 15 % to 50 %, with most mass marketers, like the guys paying for expensive TV and radio ads, averaging 35 % to 45 %.

The typical markup on Eagles, Krugerrands, Canadian Maple Leaf coins, and so on, is 3 % to 10 %.

Many dealers will take issue with this information. Admittedly, you can certainly find snippets of time where U.S. gold and /or rare coins have outperformed bullion.

But the problem is twofold:

1) The prices never take into account commissions paid, which normally eat up most, if not all, of the profit.
2) The few times I have found where $20 gold coins or other

rare coins outperformed gold were short lived, and if an investor didn't get out precisely at the top, the semi-numismatic coins generally went down, as gold either continued up or stayed somewhat steady.

In addition to the charts I have constructed, *Certified Coin Dealer Newsletter* has a coin index. This is the Dow Jones of rare coins.

Since 1990, when they started the index of twelve different coin market segments, only three have gained. The best performing coin segment has only gone up 11.8 % since 1990!

The overall market has lost over 6 % since 1990.
So, when your dealer says hold for the long term, he may be compounding your problem. There's an old saying:

You can't wait for the long term if you lose your money in the short term.

CHAPTER 10
HOW TO BUY GOLD, SILVER, AND PLATINUM BULLION

What Is Bullion?

This may sound like a silly question, but you need a firm answer before you decide whether you should be a buyer. Why do I say this?

If you've already called other dealers for gold coins or silver, you've probably been offered everything from American Eagles and Krugerrands to $20 Gold Liberties and St. Gaudens to 20 Francs, Russian Rubles, and Danzig Mermaids.

The same is true for silver. You'll be offered 90 % so-called Junk Bags, 100-ounce Bars, silver dollars, BU Bags, and maybe even a variety of foreign silver coins.

Unfortunately, many brokers will try to sell you what they make the most commission on, not what's best for your needs. Stay away from the hype and promises of quick wealth.

Beware of dealers using scare tactics to make you buy. Most importantly, stick with what you decide to buy for reasons you have determined to be important.

Bullion simply refers to actual silver or gold bars or coins, which trade at small premiums over the price of gold or silver on a daily basis. It does not include coins that have any rarity or collectible value. Bullions or bullion coins typically have a spread (the difference between what you actually pay and what you'd really get back if you sold at the same time) of 5 to 10 %, depending on the market at the time.

Simply stated, if you spend $10,000 on bullion and had to turn around and immediately resell it, you may get back $9,000 to $9,500 for it. The difference is costs, including wholesale spreads, plus a profit for the dealer.

Conversely, on rare or semi-rare coins, a $10,000 investment may get you back as little as $6,000 to $8,000. There is a higher cost of business and usually a higher markup by the dealers. This is why unscrupulous dealers will try to scare you into coins such as $20 St. Gaudens and $20 Liberty coins or supposedly rare date American Eagles. They make more money. They have lots of theories, from gold confiscation to growing rarity value. Suffice it to say, it simply puts more money in their pockets and less into yours.

As mentioned earlier, the most popular way to buy gold bullion is in bars or bullion coins. The following are most recommended and easiest to trade.

GOLD BULLION BARS:

Gold bars generally come in one-ounce, five-ounce, ten-ounce, and kilo size. The one ounce is probably most common, although the kilo bars are the most fun to handle!

Stick with the name brands: Credit Suisse, J.M. (Johnson Mathey), or Engelhard. Other brands are available, usually at a discount, but the name-brand bars will not need to be assayed or tested in most cases. They will also be the most recognized and easiest to liquidate when the time comes.

KRUGERRAND:

This one-ounce gold coin from South Africa was the first, full-ounce bullion coin.

They've been made since the 1960s and sold in the United States since gold became legal to own.

Of all the major gold coins, it is the least expensive. Usually it trades at $5 to $7 less than the other one-ounce coins. Of course, when you sell, you'll get $5 to $7 less also. They also come in fractional amounts of one-tenth ounce, one-quarter ounce, and one-half ounce.

CANADIAN MAPLE LEAF:

This coin is one of the most popular gold coins. Its selling point is the fact that it is pure .9999 gold, just like gold bars. (Older Leaf coins are only .999 fine.)

It also comes in one-tenth, one-quarter, one-half, and one-ounce sizes, as well as one-twentieth ounce.

AMERICAN GOLD EAGLES:

The U.S. Mint started producing bullion type coins in 1986 and quickly became stiff competition for the Krugerrand and Maple Leaf.

The Eagles are the most beautiful of the gold bullion coins in many people's opinion. It has been the premier bullion coin in this country.

The Eagle comes in one-tenth, one-quarter, one-half, and one ounce sizes. You can often buy the fractional pieces for close to the same premium (price of coin above the actual gold content) as the one ounce. We strongly recommend doing that when possible. It gives you the advantage of making up some of your costs if the premiums go up.

In the past, we've seen premiums go over 20 % on smaller Eagles!

CAUTION: There are dealers who will try to convince you that fractional Eagles, especially half-ounce, are rare and mark them up as much as 100 %, telling you they are great investments.

In conclusion, Eagles offer great advantages, including the possibility of increasing premiums. They are a great buy if you pay the right price (less than 10 % over gold and ideally closer to 7 % over spot price). Just don't get caught by a broker charging too much. If in doubt, call three more dealers, and they can give you the going prices and tell you if the original broker's prices are within normal ranges

BUFFALO GOLD COINS:

The Buffalo is newest addition to the U.S. Mint's offering of gold; they started minting them in 2006. The coin is .9999 fine in an attempt to compete with the Canadian Maple Leaf, which is also pure gold. They come individually wrapped in sheets of twenty coins from the Mint. They can easily be cut into single ounces by cutting the sheet but still protecting the coin. The Canadian coins often get damaged by not being wrapped or protected, so this is a good advantage for a pure gold coin, since they are very soft.

Some of the fractional coins go for large premiums because, although the plan was to make Buffaloes in all sizes, the Mint never seems to have enough of the small planchets. Thus, the smaller coins have not been made most years.

The one-ounce coin is a great way to purchase whenever you can buy them close to the same price as the Eagle. They are also defined as numismatic by the legislation that created them. This makes them a perfect coin for anyone worried about confiscation.

OTHER POPULAR GOLD COINS INCLUDE:

- Chinese Pandas
- Austrian Philharmonics
- Mexican Onzas

EUROPEAN GOLD COINS:

Often, dealers promote the odd-sized coins from Europe.

These are usually older coins that are sold as a way of combining coins that have bullion value and promise of future rarity value. Be cautious when purchasing these types of coins. In my opinion, the possibility of them becoming rare is nonexistent. These have been nothing more than bullion coins for decades, even over a century in many cases. The second problem is that they have odd amounts of gold in them, such as: .1867 ounce, .1947 ounce, or .2354 ounce, but are often sold as quarter-ounce gold coins.

While there is certainly no problem selling these coins to knowledgeable dealers or investors, it can be confusing to people not familiar with them.

The coins do not say "gold" on them, nor will they denote the amount of gold (one-tenth or one ounce), as the more modern coins do. If you buy them strictly as bullion and check prices first, there is nothing wrong with these coins if you decide you really want them. Just be aware of the drawbacks. Be informed.

Many dealers sell these coins at huge markups, sometimes as much as 100 %.

These coins include, but are not limited to:

- English Sovereigns .2354 ounce
- Swiss 20 Francs (Helvetias) .1867 ounce
- French 20 Francs and Roosters .1867 ounce
- Italian 20 Lira .1867 ounce
- German 20 Mark .1541 ounce
- Dutch 10 Guilders .1947 ounce
- Russia 5 Rubles .1244 ounce
- Austrian 10 Coronas .0980 ounce
- Austrian 1 Ducat .1109 ounce
- Austria 4 Ducat .4438 ounce
- Columbia 5 Pesos .2354 ounce
- Mexican 50 Pesos 1.2057 ounces
- Mexican 20 Pesos .4823 ounce
- Mexican 5 Pesos .1205 ounce

- Mexican 2 1/2 Pesos .0603 ounce
- Mexican 2 Pesos .0482 ounce

SILVER BULLION BARS:

Bars are generally available in one-ounce, five-ounce, ten-ounce, or one hundred-ounce sizes. When purchasing ten-ounce bars or larger, stick with JM or Engelhard bars. While off-brand bars certainly trade, they are generally discounted heavily when you resell.

Many companies manufacture different one-ounce "rounds," which are approximately the size of a silver dollar. These are very popular and tradable.

90 % SILVER BAGS:

Most commonly called "Junk Bags," these are one of the most popular ways to buy silver.

Junk bags are simply pre-1965 U.S. silver coins. Usually they contain a single denomination, whether it's dimes, quarters, or halves. Most dealers will sell bags based on face value (FV). A full bag is $1,000 face value of coins and equals 715 ounces. Generally, 90 % silver is available in $100, $250, $500, or $1,000 FV, although you can buy any quantity. This makes it very easy to trade.

Be aware that some dealers recommend bags of Walking Liberty 50 cent or BU (Uncirculated bags) as a better investment. You will pay a large premium for these specialty bags and, generally, pay a larger markup as well. Some of the higher price is simply the labor cost of sorting and grading these coins. We do not generally recommend these items unless the price is within 10 to 15 % of the price of normal bags. If silver really takes off, you will likely lose most, if not all, of the premium.

BAGS OF SILVER DOLLARS:

These can be tricky to buy and sell. They generally go for far more than the price of silver. The types and dates of the dollars affect the price, as does the condition of the coins. So, you end up with different prices for every category.

Some categories are:

- Peace Dollars
- 1921 Morgan Dollars
- Pre-1900 Morgan Dollars
- Cull Dollars

Additionally, each of the above bags, except Cull dollars, will be priced differently based on quality: very good, fine, very fine, extra fine, about uncirculated, and uncirculated.

It's a lot of work if you're simply looking for silver. You are really "skating the edge" of numismatics by buying dollars. Don't forget, as in everything else, when you create work, such as sorting by dates and quality, the markup goes higher.

As of this writing, dollar bags range from $6,500 to over $30,000, depending on the bag. Make sure this is really what you want before you buy.

U.S. SILVER EAGLE $1:

Issued by the United States since 1986, these coins have become very popular with investors and collectors.

Common dates go for $2.50 to $3.50 over spot silver price. Some of the more collectible dates go for over $30. This is because the coins are, in reality, silver dollars, so they are very attractive to collectors. The rarest of the Silver Eagles goes for about $5,400 per coin!

If you are buying simply for silver, we recommend buying the lowest-price coins, especially coins dated the current year. That gives you an outside chance of appreciation down the road. Of course, there's no guarantee of an increase, but by purchasing the lowest-priced coins, you have no additional risk.

These coins are generally sold by the roll, which is a tube of twenty coins.

We highly recommend these coins even though the premium is a bit high.

SILVER CANADIAN MAPLE LEAF:

This is the Canadian one-ounce silver coin.

There are two big differences between this and the Silver Eagle. The difference that doesn't matter is that the Canadian Maple Leaf is a $5 coin instead of a $1 coin. Both contain the same amount of silver—one ounce. Don't let the $5 Face Value fool you. It does *not* guarantee that you'll get $5 for it, as some people would have you believe. In the past, Canadian banks have refused to accept so called silver legal tender Canadian coins as currency.

The Maple Leaf coins are usually sold in sets of 10 coins per plastic sheet. It is important to keep the coins in this plastic to realize the best price when you sell.

OTHER:

Many other countries make one-ounce coins. Some even mint two-ounce and even five-ounce silver coins. Some of these are Australia, Mexico, Panama, and China. If you desire these coins, be cautious not to pay exorbitant prices.

PLATINUM BARS:

Platinum comes in different size bars, with one ounce the most popular. Stick with name brands, and you'll never have trouble. The most recognized are Engelhard, Credit Suisse, and J.M.

U.S. PLATINUM EAGLES:

One of the most popular ways of trading platinum is the U.S. Eagle Program. They come in one-ounce, one-quarter ounce, and one-tenth ounce sizes. The Face Value is $100, $50, $25, and $10, respectively. As with Gold Eagles, beware of unscrupulous dealers selling these coins for 50 to 100 % over the price of platinum!

PLATINUM CANADIAN MAPLE LEAF:

The Canadian coin is another popular way of trading platinum. They come in one-ounce, half-ounce, quarter-ounce, and tenth-ounce sizes.

SWISS TALERS:

These coins were highly promoted as a "future" collectible back in the 1980s. Like most other coins promoted this way, they have lost all of their premium value.

They now trade based on the daily price of platinum with no collector value. While not as popular as the U.S. Eagles or Canadian Maple Leaf, they are a very good choice for a one-ounce coin because of the small premium when available.

IRS AND BULLION:

Certain precious-metals products that are approved for contract trading by the CFTC will require reporting on IRS form 1099b when you sell them to a dealer. This can actually work to your advantage, since the IRS will have the appropriate paperwork to verify automatically the loss/profit information you will include on your next tax return.

These items include gold, silver, platinum, palladium bars, certain gold coins, and 90 % silver bags.

CHAPTER 11
SEVENTEEN TYPES OF COINS YOU DON'T WANT TO BUY OR HOLD

As a service to rare coin investors and the coin collecting public, I have amassed the following seventeen-point synopsis that illustrates, in my opinion, those categories of coins that do not offer significant upside potential in the foreseeable future and should, accordingly, be viewed as unattractive investments. As with anything, there is the possibility that some coins that fall in the following groups will prove to be worthwhile investments. But, as a rule, I believe the following are guidelines you should consider before making a purchase.

Whenever you are contemplating a rare coin investment, the key criteria to consider are:

- The rarity of the coin
- Its value as a recognized collectible
- Whether it is actively traded and well recognized by the network of dealers and collectors.

1) Modern coins. This group includes Jefferson 5c, Franklin 50c, Roosevelt 10c, Kennedy 50c, and most other coins that were minted after 1945. To put it bluntly, most of these coins are simply not rare and, due to their abundance and availability, have no real chance to realize any significant increase in value. There is a trend of collecting these coins in the highest grade possible. In my opinion, it may well turn out to be simply a fad.

2) New mint issues. Modern commemoratives—such as Olympic coins, the Washington 50c, White House coins, USO and other new issues—almost always experience a decline in price after the initial offering. Initially, the U.S. government sells these coins at a somewhat arbitrary price, letting the market determine the secondary value. *Dateline*, an NBC news magazine, devoted a segment of an editorial a few years ago to the dubious investment value of such coins.

Occasionally, there are coins that skyrocket, but this is virtually impossible to know ahead of time.

3) Common coins that are stuck in trading levels. Coins such as the common date MS-65 Buffalo 5c, 1938–45 MS-65 to MS-66 Mercury 10c, and common date Morgan and Peace $1 in MS-63 and MS-64 condition are not rare or collectible due to their relatively high supplies. Since the value of these coins are typically only marginally higher than the cost of grading, the minute the market does show some life, hundreds and even thousands get submitted for grading, thereby causing a glut in the market and decreasing the price back to its previous level.

4) Hoard coins. This includes such "rare treasures" as the Wells Fargo 1908 $20 St. Gaudens and Redfield $1. Initially, millions were minted. Large quantities were bagged and stored in bank vaults, private hands, or lost. The market was then determined by a supply that was kept artificially low. That is, until it was dumped on the market.

What may seem like a good price based on the previous valuation of the coin becomes a money-losing proposition once the quantity is increased by a multiple of ten to a hundred times, and the dealer network stops supporting the prices. Whenever you have an ever-increasing supply of any item and a market becomes saturated, elementary economics dictates that the value of the product will decrease significantly. Many of these hoard coins are historically significant, and you may choose to buy for this reason alone.

5) Low-population, unrecognized rarities. Certain rare date gold and Type coins are especially vulnerable to high premiums, even though they contain no corresponding market demand, meaning that the price is artificially set by the few trading in such rarities.

Coins like the 1868 1/2 10c and 1868 10c are not well recognized and, therefore, only have a slim chance of appreciating, as you must find the one-in-a-million collector actively seeking that coin. This makes for an investment that is not liquid in nature. If you want to reduce your risk and make money in the coin market, it is imperative that you stick to actively traded coins with some degree of market appeal as opposed to making emotional decisions in your portfolio strategy.

6) Low-population, low-grade coins. These coins, like the 1889 $5 Liberty in AU, for example, are not recognized or collectible. Generally speaking, the market cares little about coins of a low grade regardless of how rare they are, except for those rare examples like the 1909 SVDB cent and 1895 Morgan dollar, as well as other "super rare" collector coins. Remember that when purchasing rare coins, you are doing so with the intent of selling them one day for a profit. If a coin is so rare that it is not known and, therefore, not coveted by the market at large, you may have little chance to sell it, let alone at a profit.

7) Treasure coins. "Gold Doubloons" and "Pieces of Eight" make for great conversation but are normally poor investments. These coins are not rare, collectible, or recognized, which, as I mentioned, are the main criteria you consider when analyzing any coin purchase. Most "treasure ships" are loaded with tons of these coins. As they were the most widely used method of payment in the "New World," they were manufactured in bulk.

While they are indeed old, age has little to do with coin value and appreciation.

8) Foreign bullion-type coins. Russian 5 Rubles, Pandas, foreign Olympic coins, U.K. Proof Gold sets, proof nuggets, kilo silver coins, and a huge variety of newly minted oddities are not collectible, and you will typically have a hard time recouping your investment even if gold takes off. Their only real worth is the value of the gold contained in them, which, at "meltdown" prices, rarely exceeds their original purchase price.

9) Common coins. This category is one of the largest and most pushed by the large telemarketing firms. This category includes all grades of St. Gaudens, common Morgan dollars in MS-60 to MS-66 condition, and common Peace dollars graded at MS-60 to MS-65.

These are the favorites of brokers because huge supplies make them very cheap at wholesale. Common coins have consistently under performed in the market by a large margin, even losing value while other coins were going up.

We've already had that in bullion, and common material sorely lagged. What kind of leverage do you have over the buyer when you sell a "common" coin? They are marketed because dealers have so many of them. Over 1½ million $20 St Gaudens are graded. The fact that dealers sell common coins created a market for Europeans to dump coins on U.S. buyers.

The sad part is liquidity is usually terrible. The high bidder on the CCE (computerized trading network) will often only take ten or twenty coins at his bid. If one had Gold Eagles, the bid is generally good for hundreds if not thousands of coins.

With common coins, one gives up liquidity and appreciation while gaining no advantage over bullion coins. The only one who comes out ahead is the dealer selling them.

10) BU rolls and late-date proof sets. Proof Franklins, Washington 25c, BU Buffalo 5c rolls, Jefferson 5c rolls, Lincoln 1c rolls … all are a fluke of promotional efforts made back in the 1960s. These products are far too common to have any upside potential due to the large amounts that currently exist on the market. Although the price of silver has risen from $3.50, many rolls, like Buffalo nickels and Mercury dimes, have decreased significantly, by as much as 50 %, during the same period. Even if the prices of rare coins dramatically increase due to their quantity and availability, I would expect minimal upward movement for this class of coin.

11) California fractional gold. Although very rare and

somewhat collectible, these items are not well recognized and do not have an active trading market, thereby making them less desirable as investments for most people. Often, the spreads are so large that it becomes difficult to make money. If you simply want a fun coin to collect, these coins are certainly very historic.

12) Esoteric coins. There aren't enough buyers and, consequently, their narrow market leaves them wide open to pricing abuse. As a profit-orientated rare coin investor, the trick is to find coins that are not so common as to have little upside potential, but also not so rare as to have no market. Leave esoteric coins to the egocentric collector.

13) Patterns. Some of these coins are very collectible and do end up being profitable, although narrow markets again limit the appeal. Only a handful of experts are able to evaluate these coins accurately, and finding a collector for specific examples can be difficult. Pricing is often a problem. If you are not well connected to seriously minded collectors who deal in such coins, it is better to invest your money elsewhere.

14) Sets. Complete Sets of Coins. Many dealers will try to have you purchase coins in an attempt to complete a full or "short" set. The pitch is that once you complete a set, the coins are worth more than the sum of the coins' value. On first look, it seems like it should make sense, since you or the dealer must do all the hard work of finding the whole set.

The fact is that it almost never happens. Go no farther than looking at auction records to see the reality of this proposition. In most auctions, sets are completely broken down to individual coins. Some of the dismantled sets are ones that took a lifetime to acquire by very dedicated numismatists. I have been to many auctions where the auctioneer would take separate bids on a collection or set. The first bid would be as a set. The next would be bids individually on the coins in a set. I have never seen the set price come out equal to or more than the individual bids. The auction company is paid to get every dollar out of the collection and ends up splitting the set to maximize the price.

This happens on a regular basis.

I handled the finest known registry set of $10 Indian Head gold pieces. This was truly a one-of-a-kind set. To get the most money for it, I had to sell the coins individually.

Why?

The buyers were typically other collectors or dealers supplying their clients with coins. If one person needed a certain coin to upgrade or fill a hole in his set, he would certainly be likely to pay something extra to get what he needed. The problem was that none were willing to pay extra for every coin in the collection.

This is a selling tactic used by dealers simply to talk you into buying more coins. It's easier to lock you into future sales and usually charge you more than top dollar to finish your set. Ironically, they probably bought a lot of the coins from other sets that were being broken up.

Coin sets that dealers love to assemble for collectors include:

- $2½ Indian Heads
- Franklin Half Dollars
- Walking Liberty Half Dollars
- Gold Commemorative Coins
- Peace Dollars
- Silver Eagles

These are just a few examples of what I see most often. These are favorites, because they are fairly easy for dealers to obtain all the coins in the set.

I frequently run into investors who mistakenly think that they have a one-of-a-kind item because the set is complete.

For investment purposes, one would be better off buying only the key coins to the set so that they hold the most sought-after coins when others are building sets.

15) So-called rare date Gold and Platinum Eagles. These modern bullion coins have been the attention of several dealers. The theory is the same one that failed time after time throughout the 1980s and 1990s; namely, that the dealers could create rarities by promoting certain coins. For several years, investors were sold various "rare" bullion coins such as Pandas, Britannia's U.K. proof sets, and so on. With few exceptions, these coins are now worth only their bullion value. Investors who bought into the theory that low-mintage bullion coins would become rare lost millions of dollars.

Buying rare date Gold and Platinum Eagles is a quick way to lose money. As bullion values go up, the premium typically goes down. Furthermore, as the promoters move on to different items, the prices fall, because the false demand disappears.

If you want to gamble, buy these coins as close to bullion value as possible.

16) High-grade Proof MS-69 to 70 Coins. Most coins sold by the Mint today are produced in high grade. Randomly grading modern coins such as Eagles, Olympic $5, any modern proof set or other commemorative will produce a huge number of MS or PR-69 to 70 coins. That's the typical grade straight from the Mint. So, while these high grades are very rare in coins produced prior to the 1950s, they are average for modern coins sold by the Mint since the 1990s. Modern Proof coins, including American Eagles, Kennedy Halves, and Statehood Quarters are not rare, even in high grades. Many show low "populations" simply because no one has bothered to send coins to the grading services. Given the millions of coins minted, many high grades will surface as dealers send them for certification.

This is another "created" market. The dealers simply buy the modern coins and send them to the various grading services. Their cost for grading is generally under $10 a coin. The coins that grade out at 69 or 70 are then marked up 50 to 300 % and sold as investments.

In my opinion, the secondary, or resale, market has not developed because of the inexhaustible supply. If a dealer needs more, he simply sends more to get certified.

Interestingly enough, in recent purchases, I have been getting coins graded MS-69 for $5 *less* than non-graded coins. I have even seen buy-back offers from dealers who sold the high-grade Buffalo coins for only about $35 over spot (the value of the gold).That's less than an ungraded coin.

17) First-strike and early release coins. In the past few years, dealers really jumped on a completely arbitrary designation to add to their profit margins. In fact, the U.S. Mint actually reported on its Web site that no such thing as a first strike exists on the modern Eagles or Buffaloes.

In the past, a first strike was more of a ceremonial coin that was documented and presented by the Mint.

Today, there is no way to tell the First Strike from the last. The Mint uses very high standards and goes to extremes on quality control. In fact, they report that only fifteen hundred coins are made on a single die and only three hundred to five hundred on a proof Eagle die for just that reason.

There were some legal problems, I believe, with the "First Strike" designation. The U.S. Mint published an article stating there was no such thing as a First Strike. This forced the grading services to abandon that designation and instead, the services designated coins as Early Release.

In my opinion, it's a complete joke. The only criteria the grading services use is the date on the packaging from the Mint. This is not something you want to pay extra for.

I believe this is a totally contrived market that allows dealers to make a larger markup on bullion coins.

I can tell you for a fact that when I sell these coins back into the market, they do not command any premium whatsoever, even from the guys who are touting them.

SECTION III

THE MYTHS, LIES, AND UNTRUTHS OF THE RARE COIN MARKET

Rare coin dealers perpetuate misconceptions about coins. This section looks into the workings of the rare coin market. If you own or are thinking of owning rare coins, this is essential.

CHAPTER 12
COIN DEALERS—THE GOOD, THE NOT SO GOOD, AND THE UGLY

Coin dealers can be classified into three groups:

1. **The honest, smart, and experienced dealers.** These ethical dealers charge a fair commission, have done their homework, and will do their very best to make their clients money (but even they cannot guarantee a profit).
2. **The well-meaning dealers** who believe the facts they are giving you are correct. But their facts may be wrong or inaccurate! They're not unethical; they just haven't done the research, are inexperienced, or both. They seldom make their clients money.
3. **The dishonest unethical "hucksters."** These dealers, promoters, and/or telemarketers will lie to you and pressure you into bad investments.

There are honest, ethical, and smart dealers who have ridden the ups and downs with full integrity and an impressive degree of professionalism in their dealings with their clients—and our hats are off to them. It's not their fault that the market dropped. They usually honor their word and will buy back coins at market prices. However, these honest and ethical dealers are rarely the people calling you on the phone every week with a "hot" deal.

Those who bought from the truly great dealers are not going to relate to this section of the book.

I travel fifty states, and I'm in the field three to five days a week, almost every other week of the year. Therefore, I am fairly confident that I am accurate in my assessment of what reality looks like in the rare coin world, what you need to know and be prepared for, and what you need to understand so you can talk with and understand the language of coin dealers.

In early 2005, I visited a schoolteacher who had recently been let go. She was basically down to her last pennies ... yet, she did have her "rare" coin portfolio to fall back on. Apparently, she bought these coins from an aggressive, LA-based dealer through his radio talk show. Since she bought, gold had gone up almost 70 % and certainly, as she had been informed by the numismatic expert who called, her "rare" coins would follow suit.

Even though gold had gone up so dramatically, her $16,000 investment in rare coins had decreased to $9,200! She mentioned something to the effect of, "I knew I was in trouble when I searched the classifieds and the same company I had bought from was advertising a sales position where there was 'no coin experience necessary'."

I wish I could say that this was an isolated incident ... but its not and is one I hear repeated at least a few times per month from people I visit. One elderly person spent his entire life savings, $150,000, for coins that were determined to be worth only $1,800! The only good news here is that the firm was indicted in New York for wire fraud and running a boiler room telemarketing scheme. Hopefully, this gentleman, as well as the thirteen other elderly individuals who invested in a similar manner, will receive some kind of help from the government in getting their money back. It's not always that bad, but most coin companies that heavily market to investors hire salespeople based on their selling ability, not their numismatic knowledge.

These salespeople are rarely numismatists. They are employees who, in their last job, may have sold timeshares, long distance, vitamins, bullion, whatever. They tell you what their sales manager tells them to say. They may sound like they know what they're talking about, but that's only because they're trained in what to say to make the sale. All most care about is their commission check.

When you're investing in coins, you want to deal with

companies known in the industry for their expertise, and where you can deal with true numismatic experts. You want companies that sell individual coins, not just promoters of $20 gold pieces, silver dollars, sovereigns, and the similar coins that so many dealers have been hawking to investors the past twenty-plus years.

CHAPTER 13
THE SEVEN MYTHS OF COIN INVESTING

There are five main myths of coin investing that trap most investors. Dealers, even those who are honest if not naïve, have circulated these myths for decades. They are absolutely untrue, but dealers who sell to the inexperienced investor commonly use each one today.

Myth #1: "Buy and Hold"

"Put your coins in your bank box, and don't even think about selling them for ten or twenty years. Save them until you retire; you'll be glad you did."

In the 1960s and 1970s, this was a common myth, even among the best dealers and savvy investors. It has since been proven untrue. Today, it's nothing but a line of bunk, commonly espoused by dealers. Sometimes, they use it when selling you coins they hope they never see again. They often say it when you try selling it back to them. In either case, it's almost always a sign you own losers.

A coin you forget until retirement might be worth a fortune when you blow the dust off in your golden years. But, based on the past twenty-eight years, it's more likely you'll find an unpleasant surprise. Either the coin won't be the good investment you were told it would be, or you'll find that the market had peaked in the meantime, and the coin is worth much less than you could have sold it for earlier.

Markets don't pay attention to your retirement date or the arbitrary ten or twenty year period you decide to hold your coins. You need to keep your eye on the market, even if you intend to hold your coins for decades, just as you would with your other investments.

And just like stocks, all coins go through cycles. Most expert investors sell hot coins into the market when prices are high and they feel they're about to become overpriced. They buy them back when the prices go down again and they find coins that they feel have sound potential. If they find that a coin they own isn't a good investment, they get rid of it even at a low price, take their lumps, and use the proceeds to invest in something else. Often, they just put the money in the bank until another good opportunity arises.

The worst thing you can do is hang onto a bad investment rather than face taking a loss. Too many people do this and almost always end up in even worse shape. If you're holding some poor investments and you're in your thirties, forties, or early fifties, maybe you think you can afford to play the "hold and hope" game. But it's nothing more than wishful thinking to think that time alone will heal your investment wounds. I know thousands of investors in their seventies, eighties, and nineties who once thought like that, but today agree with me and would tell you you're making a mistake.

Myth #2: Rare Coins Never Go Down

This is another myth from the 1960s, 1970s, and 1980s, even among the most honest dealers, that has proven to be unquestionably false. Dealers often tell new investors that rare coins never go down. If you've been an investor for more than a few years, odds are you are painfully aware that this is anything but true.

Unless you pay face value, there's no such thing as a no-risk coin. Just like stocks, bonds, and real estate, every coin, no matter how great it is, goes through hot and cold markets. If a dealer ever tells you otherwise, hang up the phone, commit their name to memory, and never talk to them again.

Myth #3: Doomsday Buying

The first thing that bothered me both in my personal investing and the coin market overall was this: Starting in the late 1970s, most investors, including me, were investing with one thing in mind—

disaster.

That's right. People were planning only for economic collapse, inflation, and political chaos. It's easy to get caught up in the doomsday scenarios and to be blindsided because of tunnel vision. But there are many dangers in a doomsday investment strategy.

1. Dealers may use the emotional weight of the doomsday scenario to push investors into making a decision. Many dealers firmly believe that economic disaster is imminent and will communicate this urgency to you. You may then find yourself investing more than you intended or investing in something you have not fully researched.
2. Doomsday scenarios also enable outrageous markups. In the year or so leading up to Y2K, dealers could (and many would) literally name their price for "survival coins."
3. Investing for doomsday places you, as the investor, in a no-win situation. Think about it. If disaster happens and your worst fears are realized, odds are that your coins will be worthless, because there will not be an economy that can support the sale and exchange of rare coins. We all have the image in our head of desperate people sewing valuables into the hems of garments prior to fleeing a country in chaos. If being prepared to flee the United States at a moment's notice is important to you, by all means, go for it! Buy as many high-value, low-bulk rare coins as you can get your hands on. If, on the other hand, you feel that it's unlikely you'll have to flee a totalitarian United States in the near future, reign in your doomsday paranoia as your sole investment strategy.
4. If you always have your attention focused on a future doomsday, you're missing out on important opportunities today. Sadly, there are tens of thousands, if not hundreds of thousands, of people who spent the last twenty-five years buying coins to save them from doomsday. They made no other plans for their future. They missed out on the high

interest rates of the 1980s, the amazing stock market of the 1990s, twenty-five years of excellent real estate opportunities, and now they are sitting on coins worth a fraction of what they were when they bought them ... and living on Social Security.

Buying some gold or rare coins as insurance or even speculation for uncertain times can make sense. Banking your entire future on gold, silver, or rare coins does not.

Myth #4: Your Dealer Is Looking Out for Your Best Interest

Many dealers consider me bad for the industry because (as you'll see throughout this book) I tell collectors and investors what I know about coin investing. They don't want anyone to explain the inner workings of the coin industry. They don't want you to know that in my experience, over 95 % of coin investors lose money, or that most of the large dealers are interested in selling coins to anyone and everyone they can. It bothers them that my opinions are so different than theirs.

Many brokers care only about their hefty markups and commissions. This is why they make up outrageous stories and make spectacular promises.

How can dealers who mark-up coins 50 to 100 % or more possibly have your best interest at heart?

Certainly, dealers are in business to make money, but few have the incentive to make you money. Sure, they'd like to see the market roar ahead like it did in 1989, but they know they can't count on it. They must make as much as possible on every transaction, because they know most buyers won't be buying for long.

Most dealers care only about their financial security ... not yours.

Myth #5: It's Easy to Make Money in Rare Coins

This is out-and-out false. Yes, you can make money in coins, but the odds are highly stacked against you unless you know what you're doing.

The good news is if you're losing money in coins, by reading this book, you're going to learn how to minimize your losses and even turn around your investment. And if you're considering investing in coins, or you're one of the very few coin investors who is making money without knowing much about the coin market, you're going to learn how to avoid the mistakes that plague most coin investors.

Myth #6: Rare Coins Are Not Reportable

Dealers lead you to believe that when you make money in rare coins, you do not have to report the gain. I guess they get away with this claim because their clients never do make money, so they never confront the IRS with this.

The reason this is misquoted is that as a dealer, we don't report to the IRS. However, by law, you are required to report any gain on your taxes. This is no different for rare coins than most other bullion coins. Dealers will conveniently forget to tell you that the same reporting requirements are true for Gold and Silver Eagles, Buffaloes, and a large variety of foreign gold coins.

What they are telling you is that you can lie and they won't tell on you.

Myth #7: Rare Coins Are Safe from Confiscation

This is perhaps the most abused scare tactic out there. It is used daily by dealers to sell high-priced U.S. gold coins instead of bullion gold coins. I can't even estimate how many hundreds of times people have told me they called a dealer to buy gold but were switched into rare or semi-numismatic gold coins because they were safer.

Dealers continue to interpret this past executive order in many self-serving ways. I discuss this more in further chapters. I am currently writing a book just on this topic.

The assumption is that if a coin is numismatic, it would be exempt from confiscation if that order were still on the books, but it was repealed by Gerald Ford. Interestingly, there is a really great book that covers this part of history and documents what happened. The name of the book is Double Eagle, by Alison Frankel.

In it, there are documented cases of the government actually going after dealers and fining and forcibly confiscating coins. Their idea of "collectable" was very different than what is being promoted by dealers today.

I was shocked to find out that they confiscated coins from the early 1800s, Draped Bust coins, and others that were even at that time more than one hundred years old. If this was OK by the standards of what the government considers, "of special value to collectors,", then there is no hope that common $20 St. Gaudens or Liberties would be exempt.

Additionally, some of the very coins dealers are telling you not to buy, or worse yet, trade out of, are specifically defined in legislation as numismatic. The legislation that created the Gold Eagle, Buffalo, and most modern coins specifically defines them as numismatic or rare coins. That should make them much safer than coins such as the old $20s, which were actually confiscated the first time!

If you care to look for yourself, you can find the information on the Mint's Web site or on the Internet. The Gold Bullion Act of 1985, or Title 31 sec 2A of Section 5111 of the U.S. code, states, "For purposes of section 5132(a)(1) of this title, all coins minted under this subsection shall be considered to be numismatic items."

CHAPTER 14
THE HOARDS

It's been very common over the past four decades for huge hoards of coins to appear in the market. They come from shipwrecks, government vaults, banks, or even individual families. They have included the Redfield Dollars, Carson City Dollars, Wells Fargo $20, and SS *Central America*, just to name a few of the multimillion dollar hoards. Dealers and marketers love to promote hoard coins because:

A) There are a lot of coins to sell
B) They are usually surrounded by publicity
C) They tend to have a great historical story that goes with them

Unfortunately, in some cases, they are often promoted as great investments.

Some promoters have consistently tried to defy the simple economic principle of supply and demand. Even though they have found thousands or tens of thousands of coins, they must somehow sell the coins without flooding the market.

Does anyone really believe that finding huge amounts of anything makes it more rare?

In the mid-1990s, approximately thirty thousand 1908 $20 St. Gaudens were found. The hoard was named the Wells Fargo Hoard. Dealers publicized, promoted, and sold the story behind these now common, although high-quality, coins.

The sheer number finally impacted the price, and it soon fell by over 60 %! In fact, according to my sources, in 2004, some of the high-grade coins (MS-66) remained unsold.

Another popular hoard was the SS *Central America* coins.

The *Central America* was a ship that sunk in 1857 and was

laden with newly minted gold coins and bullion. It was discovered in 1988 and salvaged. It was marketed in the beginning of 2000. It was really quite exciting, and I personally had a chance to view many of the salvaged items in California. From a historical standpoint, it was quite extraordinary.

The coins were marketed by just a handful of well-known and reputable dealers with a blitz of publicity. Each coin was sold in an attractive presentation case, and the buyer usually received a book about the SS *Central America*. This was probably the most exciting hoard I've ever seen.

While certainly a find of great historic value and a treasure (no pun intended) for collectors, it remains to be seen if they will turn out to be great investments. It should be noted that these coins were sold based on their historic value for the most part, not as investments.

If you decide you really just want a coin from any hoard because of the history, not investment potential, there is nothing wrong with buying. In fact, that is the most compelling reason to buy. You should wait a year or two, and you may save a substantial amount of money.

CHAPTER 15
DEALERS "NEW MATH": Calculating Markups

You may be angry, offended, or depressed by this new math.

Many investors never bother to ask what the spread or markup is before they buy coins.

When they do ask, they frequently get an answer that only makes sense when it's time to sell.

Investors have told me that when they bought, they were told there was a 28 % (or more) spread. Many assumed the coin had to go up 28 % to break even or the coin was marked up 28 %. This is not correct.

Using the "new math," the coin is actually marked up 40 %. A 28 % spread means the dealer paid 28 % less than the sales price.

Do the math yourself to verify this. If a $1,000 coin is sold at a 28 % spread, it means the client paid $1,000 and the dealer paid 28 % less, or $720. That's not a 28 % markup. For example, use the same coin, for which a dealer paid $720. A 28 % markup would mean the coin is sold for $922, not $1,000.

$720 x 28% = $202. $202 (the 28 % markup) + $720 (cost) = $922

Again, if you looked at the $720 coin and added 40 %, the coin would be retailed at $1,008, basically, the same price as the 28 % spread.

$720 x 40% = $288. $288 (40 % markup) + $720 (cost) = $1,008

I know, it's a little confusing, but it's important, and it will cost you money if you don't understand.

Typically, when a dealer gets caught, he will simply try to

talk a client into selling tomorrow, tomorrow, tomorrow. They will avoid giving a bid price and simply try to get the poor investor to wait. Often, they will claim the market is just getting ready to boom or some event is just on the horizon. Sometimes, they will even try to convince you that Congress is about to pass a new law that will benefit coins.

A popular one has been to imply that Congress is about to allow coins in IRAs again. While there certainly has been an effort to get coins reinstated, don't hold your breath. Coins have not been allowed in an IRA since the early 1980s. As of this writing, the only thing you can put in an IRA is bullion. Many times, if the dealer is pushed to give you a current price on your coins, he may quote you a price that's 20 to 30 % higher than market in an attempt to cover up his original profit. They will hope this pacifies you and that you decide not to sell. Then, if you still want to sell, they again will give you reasons not to or just say they aren't buying right now. This can all be avoided by simply understanding the markup in the first place.

CHAPTER 16
THE NEXT DEPRESSION ... WILL YOU NEED TO BARTER?

Many dealers were advocating buying coins so that when the economy and dollar fall apart, you can trade for the necessities. Unfortunately, they often recommend odd foreign coins or collectibles.

We have been a major recession for quite a while. Rare coins never have done well in recessions or depressions. The only reason they moved with gold in 1979 was because the gold dealers were pushing rare coins. Today, most of the gold investing is done electronically on ETFs, funds, or stocks. Therefore, the physical gold market doesn't bleed over to rare coins.

Try this one test for yourself. Take a gold coin and tell someone you lost your wallet and you need some money to fly home. See if anybody will buy that gold coin from you. Before Y2K, I tried offering a $20 St. Gaudens gold coin. I was offering them at $250. Gold was $300 an ounce. I didn't get a single taker.

However, when I took a U.S. silver dollar, which was worth $5 to $10, I had no problem. There were lots of people who said, "I don't know what that's worth, but that's neat. I recognize it. I'll give you $5 or $10." People will take a chance for $5 or $10 but not for $200, $300, or over $1,000.

Dealers don't want you to use common sense when thinking about this "barter" situation. They want to play on your fear. They want you to buy coins they can mark up heavily like rare coins, $20 Gold, or even foreign coins like Swiss and French Francs. Or worse yet, certified bullion coins like Eagles and Buffaloes.

If you ever get in a situation where you need to barter with gold, you will need to keep it simple. Most Americans will have no idea what a rare or semi-rare coin is worth. Most will not recognize a Swiss 20 Franc or a British Sovereign. These coins don't even say "gold" on them. Do you think that people will care if your Eagle is MS-69 or 70? Do you think it really affects what the gold is worth? Of course not. And forget about selling or trading rare coins. They'll be spending them.

Asking someone to simply trust you as far as gold, gold content, and value could be a tough sell. I don't think it is a good idea for you to complicate a trade in a crisis situation. You could end up with no trade or much worse. If you truly are concerned, stick with small amounts of silver coins (10c, 25c, 50c, or $1), which people may recognize and accept. Small U.S. gold coins, such as one-tenth ounce Eagles or quarter-ounce, Eagles also fit the bill. They are less valuable than a full ounce. They say right on the coin, "1/10 oz. pure gold" or "1/4 oz. pure gold." They are minted in the United States and denoted in English. Best of all, these items have small markups if you purchase them correctly.

Of course, brokers hate them because they can only make 3 to 10 % profit, not the 35 % plus to which they are accustomed.

If there ever is such global, economic chaos that people have to use gold and silver coins to buy the basic necessities of life, we'd all have bigger problems than how much gold we have to barter with—although it certainly wouldn't hurt to have some gold on hand.

If you do want to buy coins or gold as a hedge against this catastrophic event, buy it in small denominations, because you'll probably be more interested in buying a chicken than a new Mercedes Benz. (For information and details on buying gold bullion, silver, and platinum, see chapter 10.)

To prepare yourself for this scenario, you should buy one-tenth ounce gold coins such as Eagles, Maple Leaf coins, or any of a number of bullion one-tenth ounce gold coins. Expect to pay up to a 20 % premium for the coin. Also, consider some junk silver or 90 % silver coins minted prior to 1964. Again, be careful. Some dealers will sell you all different varieties to charge you more. If they start talking about bags of Walking Liberty half-dollars or uncirculated coins or Mercury Dimes, they are likely adding more to their markup.

CHAPTER 17
NEW NAME, NEW RULES

It's not uncommon for dealers to change the name of their company. It's also not uncommon for people who need to sell the coins they purchased from the original company to call the new company for help. It's also not uncommon for the dealer to say that they can't honor old guarantees because the company has changed names.

What they don't say, but actually mean in many cases, is that they had so many lawsuits and so many complaints they had to close that corporation and start over under a new corporate name. Or, they wanted to get out from under some unforeseen liability. And by the way, that means that any guarantee from the old company, implied or otherwise, doesn't exist.

And they'll change the name only slightly. Maybe it was "Such and Such Ltd." Now, it's "Such and Such Group." So, it'll sound almost the same, but it's not.

To add further insult, you'll notice that the broker or dealer talking to you has not even a tinge of remorse, guilt, culpability, or responsibility for this legal maneuver, even though he or she was the one who sold the coins to you.

I talked to an investor who spent $64,000 on a single $10 Liberty coin. Two years later (after the company changed ownership), the broker told him it was only worth $3,600. The broker said the previous company really cheated him. It's bad enough that dealers will use a name change to deny any legal or moral responsibility for the advice they gave you, but what is even more unconscionable is the way they will use that name change as an excuse to sell you more!

The dealer will excitedly proclaim the investment strategies offered by the new company and then they'll go on to say, "So that junk that the old company sold you should be traded into something else."

Also, I noticed as gold has gone up, more and more "brokers" have branched out on their own. They see the good market and fat markups being made by the company and decide to do it themselves. Do you really want to be the person they use to learn the business?

My experience has been that that many of these offshoots have little money, experience, ethics (they stole your name from their employer), or longevity.

I have also noticed that some of the newcomers will use a name very similar to a long-standing company.

The only thing the new upstarts won't do is give you cash. But if you want to let them talk you into making a trade again, they'll happily take their inflated commissions again. I know a man who worked with one broker who went through four companies and four trades. He managed to take $80,000 and whittle it down to $24,000… just through these trades. "When were you going to figure out that you should stop dealing with that particular broker?" I asked. The client responded, "Well, I don't deal with him anymore, because he's out of the business." It wouldn't have stopped until his capital was eroded to zero. I've seen it happen time after time. I had my head handed to me in the stock market believing what I wanted to hear and believing that brokers spoke the truth and were looking out for my best long-term interest. If legitimate stockbrokers are guilty of selling investors questionable stocks or bonds to pocket commissions, what do you think some unregulated brokers in the coin business are doing?

The Security Exchange Commission (SEC) polices the stock market and investment banking. Stockbrokers need to operate under the watchful eye of the government, their own industry watchdog group, and the SEC. The SEC or any other government agency to any great degree does not regulate coins. There is no industry watchdog to monitor illegal or unethical practices.

Maybe as a result of this, the regulation of the coin industry has begun.

CHAPTER 18
MAKE SURE YOUR DEALER IS FOR REAL

Frequently, dealers will not belong to major coin organizations such as American Numismatic Association, Professional Numismatic Guild, Professional Coin Grading Service, or Numismatic Guaranty Corp., to name a few of the major ones.

Their reasons range from the organizations being too political to having their own in-house graders. Dealers who don't belong and don't sell certified coins when selling investment or high-quality coins should be avoided at all costs.

I should also mention that there are reputable dealers who sell ungraded (uncertified coins) to collectors. Many true collectors are comfortable grading their own coins and enjoy handling them and assembling sets. But for most investors, it is an unwise move if they are buying coins that are rare.

Although few organizations do police their ranks, there are exceptions. The Professional Numismatic Guild (PNG) is the premier coin organization in the country. They do a fairly thorough background check of finances and dealer relationships. All members must sign and adhere to a strict code of ethics. Members must also answer to and submit to penalties in arbitrations handled by the PNG on behalf of disgruntled clients.

The American Numismatic Association (ANA), also has a code of ethics and can apply pressure to dealers.

The premier grading services, Professional Coin Grading Service (PCGS) and Numismatic Guaranty Corp. (NGC), do prescreening of applicants as well.

Some companies will claim their in-house graders are tougher than these reputable third-party grading services. I have found that the more likely scenario is that their coins are so poor that the services would never even grade them.

In case you don't understand how the most reputable grading services operate, understand that they operate totally independently and, therefore, hire independent graders, not dealers. They assess coins and assign the quality based on the evaluation of their expert graders.

It turns coins into more of a commodity, which has a national market that coin dealers maintain. If you have PCGS or an NGC coin, it makes it possible for you to call a dealer to get an accurate idea of its true value.

Before the advent of the professional coin grading services, all dealers self-graded. Many coins sold turned out to be two grades lower than represented.

That is not to say there weren't some very good people out there. Not surprisingly, most of the services' founders were selling quality coins before submitting themselves to consensus grading.

But the point was that it was all subjective, not objective. It was all singular, instead of a consensus.

You want to run, not walk, from that situation.

Even if you were dealing with an honest dealer, you would be foolish to rely strictly on the grade of a single dealer in today's market. Not only do you jeopardize the liquidity (because no other dealer will buy the coin based on another's subjective opinion), you also take a huge and often expensive risk.

The difference in price for a simple one-grade discrepancy can be hundreds, thousands, even tens of thousands of dollars.

The certified coins, such as PCGS, ANACS, and NGC, greatly reduce this risk.

Beware of most other grading companies. Very few have the reputation or following of the top three. In fact, most of the others are outright detrimental to you.

The important part really is that thousands of professional dealers will buy PCGS and NGC coins, no questions asked. That's what you need when it's time to sell. Otherwise, you're hoping one dealer can provide a market when reality tells you that it takes many. Even if your one dealer does provide a resale market for his coins, chances are he will be unable to handle any large quantity if more than a handful of clients are selling. Remember, unless he has new clients coming to him to buy, even he must rely on the overall market for liquidity.

I met a client in Detroit, who told me about the coins he had purchased. Unfortunately, the coins were dealer graded, not certified by any recognized grading service like PCGS, NGC, or ANACS. As mentioned earlier, these services provide unbiased third-party grading of the quality of coins and are universally accepted across the country by literally thousands of dealers.

The dealer he bought from had a list of reasons he did not like the grading services. They ranged from not liking the owners of the grading services to not liking the holders in which the coins were sealed.

I immediately recognized the company and knew what to expect. Inspecting the coins verified my fear. Every coin had been cleaned, polished, or repaired! Each of these is very detrimental to the value of any coin. While he had spent over $40,000, his investment was only worth $5,600! Worse still, the coins were so damaged that none of the major grading services would even evaluate and grade them.

CHAPTER 19
HOW RARE IS TOO RARE?

There are coins that are so rare and esoteric that their values are almost never listed. The market is usually so thinly traded that only a handful of people know the true value of the coin.

If a coin only trades hands once every five years, for example, how do you track the price? Add to the equation that coin buyers are very private about their transactions, and you can see how hard it is to track esoteric coins. I have personally sold coins in the $100,000 to $300,000 categories with the stipulation from the buyer or buyer's representative that I not be allowed to let the selling price become public knowledge.

Please keep in mind that there are exceptions to this rule, as there are with any. If you are an avid investor or collector, some areas may be very profitable and enjoyable. But for the average investor, these areas can become a real trap.

There are many areas that fall into this category, coins that are truly rare but have a thin market and, therefore, few collectors.

They include items such as:

1. Patterns

These are trial and experimental pieces made by the Mint to see what a coin may look and feel like. Most of these never turn out to be circulation coinage. They are like concept cars—only one in a hundred are produced.

However, there are thousands of different Patterns out there, all with small mintages. Unless you are willing to immerse yourself in this area and learn as much as possible, I would recommend you stay away from these coins.

2. California Gold

These coins were made from the mid-1800s until 1882. Because of the shortage of coinage in the West, private minters made 25c, 50c, and $1 coins out of gold. They were tiny coins, and there is a huge variety of them. While they are indeed historically significant, they are hard to price and sell. Again, unless you are willing to get deeply involved as a collector, I would stay away from these.

3. Super High-Grade MS-69, MS-70 Coins

These are condition rarities, and again there is little pricing info available. There has been a recent push to buy the best coins or collections available and register them. It's exciting, because it is a brand new trend. However, it may only be a trend; we simply don't know yet. And while certain modern coins are selling for tens of thousands of dollars, we have no idea what the future holds. I would classify this as truly speculative. The high-grade MS-68 and MS-69 or Pr-69 and Pr-70 that are being marketed to investors are usually the modern commemoratives or Eagle Bullion coins. These may be all right, if you pay a small premium. But don't pay 50 % to 100 % more for high-grade bullion coins. Realistically, that's all the Gold and Platinum Eagle coins are! You must realize that with modern methods of making coins, they are not that unusual even in "69" and "70" grades.

Graded bullion coins are one of the areas of the market that dealers are selling like crazy. There is a good reason for it: they make huge markups! It's insane to pay two to three times the price of gold for a bullion coin, no matter what the grade. This is nothing but a way for dealers to sell you something on which they can make money. I have found no reliable resale market for these coins. In my opinion, they are nothing more than the newest way to overcharge the gold buying public. Sure, there are a few high auction prices on a very few select coins, but you are not going to get these prices. Unless you are the end buyer, you are going to lose money.

People who bought graded Platinum Eagle years ago, when platinum was $500 an ounce, are only now breaking even at almost $2,000 an ounce instead of showing the tremendous profits to which they were entitled. All because of greedy dealers.

No wonder most people never come back to the coin market a second time!

4. Undiscovered Rarities

Some dealers claim to have found coins that are rare, but the collectors have yet to discover them. I've heard this explanation since I was a kid, collecting in the 1960s.

What he or she is saying is that the other dealers out there who basically live, eat, and breathe coins, who look at maybe a thousand or ten thousand coins a week, travel all over the country to coin shows, and who pay thousands of dollars to be on various exchanges and look at all the data and have confidential connections, have never discovered this coin.

They are trying to sell a coin that, for some reason, collectors have never grown emotional about or, worse yet, dealers have been unable to promote. Many times, they're selling coins that are one hundred to one hundred fifty years old. The reality is, if collectors haven't discovered them in one hundred fifty years, why are they going to discover them next year? What's going to change? What phenomenon of events or of awareness is going to take place that's going to transform them?

Look at the history of these "undiscovered" rarities. Throughout the 1970s and 1980s, a few major telemarketers promoted everything from rolls of cents, nickels, and dimes to Mexican Pesos to Swiss 20 Francs and British Sovereigns. Many of these "rarities" now sell for 20 % of the original sale price. The rare Mexican Pesos sell for about $8 today, even though they were originally sold as an up-and-coming rarity for $16 to $19 each! The so-called "rare" gold sovereigns and 20 Francs are down over 50 % from retail prices charged in the 1980s (even with gold at sixteen-year highs).

One of the largest dealers in the country has revived marketing of Swiss 20 franc coins. They get sales from TV- and radio-sponsored ads and sell to trusting people with similar political views. These people are paying prices as much as 90% over current market for a bullion coin.

A companion statement, which has been very popular in the last few years, has to do with bullion coins. Some dealers like to offer bullion coins as the next rarities. They are typically selling the new American bullion coins, the Gold Eagles, and the Platinum Eagles. Usually, they are graded coins, which lends a degree of credibility to the pitch.

The pitch is something like this: "The government sells these as bullion, but look at the mintage on this rare—ounce of gold or platinum—they only made X number of these." Then the dealers sell those bullion coins as rare coins at a price of as much as 100 % or more above listed prices. On top of that, PCGS or NGC has graded these as cream of the crop MS-69 or 70.

Many people I've met bought Platinum Eagles from these brokers when Platinum was only $350 to $400 an ounce. But, because of the markups, these coins still haven't broken even, even though Platinum has quadrupled! The brokers continue to tell them they're rare, and collectors are going to decide to collect them when they discover them.

There is also a new wave of foreign coins being marketed. In fact, I have been told that certain foreign mints will take special orders for coins from marketers and produce whatever is requested.

Today, dealers are simply using the same tactics with different coins. The American Eagles are one common item, but I am seeing more and more foreign coins sold this way. Everything from silver kilo coins to five-ounce gold coins are being marketed as the next rarities.

It looks like the lessons of the 1980s will have to be learned again by new investors.

It's not that any of these dealers are necessarily crooks; it's just that they don't learn from history.

As a side note, please remember, if you are buying for bullion value, the various Eagle coins can be an excellent purchase. You must make sure, though, you are only paying a small premium over the bullion value.

We all want to believe. Many of us came from an environment where you controlled your own investing, and it worked, so you wanted to ascribe the same values, the same professionalism, same honesty, and same accuracy (many dealers think they're honest, but they're not accurate). A lot of times, the brokers don't even realize the legal manipulation they're perpetrating.

They think that selling these coins, even at the high markup, is acceptable, permissible and honorable, as long as people will buy them.

SECTION IV

GOVERNMENT AND YOUR INVESTMENT

Much is made about the fact that coins and bullion are under the radar screen. Change is coming to our industry.

CHAPTER 20
REGULATION ON THE WAY

The freedom of the coin market has been touted as one of the great advantages for investors. For the past two and a half decades, dealers have told investors that coins are private, unregulated, and below the government's radar.

This has appealed to a large number of people who want to have some private assets. It especially appeals to those who are worried about too much government and specifically buy "hard assets" as a hedge against the dollar and uncertainty. The government has slowly waded into this market.

he new health care bill has a provision that has passed into law as of this writing. It will require all sales over $600 to be reported on form 1099 to the IRS. If not repealed, it will crush the coin market and make virtually every transaction reportable. You won't be able to sell a single St. Gaudens or $20 Liberty without a 1099. The government is desperate to pay for the new health care bill, and they see this as a way to do it. I will keep our Web site, americanfederal.com, updated on this development. The reporting requirement goes into effect in 2012.

It just shows that even though one may buy coins under the assumption they are not reportable, the government can easily change it. Too many dealers sell coins under the ruse that the nonreportability of coins can't change.

Dealers must report certain purchases of gold bullion, Krugerrands, and Canadian Maple Leaf coins, as well as many silver and platinum coins, to name a few. When dealers purchase certain items and/or quantities, they are required to report the sale to the IRS.

Also, when a dealer receives more than $10,000 cash from any investor within one year's time, there is a mandatory reporting. It is sure to get much more stringent under the Patriot Act, as terrorism is used more and more as an excuse to monitor any financial transaction.

Already dealers must, "Know their clients." It's a phrase the government uses that means dealers must make an effort to know who is buying and why. "Suspicious" transactions must be reported, and certain people's heritage and citizenship may require further inquiry and reporting to the government.

Finally, the biggest threat to the coin market has apparently been breached in New York. In response to numerous complaints about "boiler room" coin operations, the governor has fought back by requiring certain dealers to be treated as licensed security dealers.

Laws put in place in the early 1930s are being more liberally interpreted to include everything from rare coins, vintage wines and whiskeys to orange groves in the government's realm of regulation.

No longer would your coin dealer be able to guide you or tell you when to buy or sell. Any dealer claiming to do that in the future may be putting himself in a precarious position.

This virtually puts dealers out of business. All but the largest dealers would be forced to close up shop should this trend spread. The coin and bullion markets would shrink and be run by a handful of dealers at that point.

It's a very unsettling trend. It may sound like regulation will protect buyers, but it may actually make the market less liquid and less viable for those striving to protect their money.

Regulation in various forms is here, and it's growing. While it certainly is beneficial in many ways, it makes it harder and harder on the coin industry, which has been in decline since 1990.

The "Analysts"

The past few years have brought government investigators and class-action lawsuits against numerous stock brokerage houses across the country.

The charges were that the so-called "analysts" promoted stocks and gave brokers bonuses for selling these stocks, which the company had an interest in selling. So, even though the company knew prices were up only because they were promoting it, they recommended that investors buy. Often, the reports given by the analysts were paid for by the same company trying to unload the stock. Worse yet was the fact that not only were the reports one sided, painting a rosy picture, but many times the brokerage already owned the stock at substantially lower prices and was simply unloading to make a profit.

Of course, none of these analysts gave "sell" recommendations until the stock had lost most of its value.

So, What Does This Have To Do with Coins?

It doesn't take much imagination to see an exact parallel in the coin market. It's happened over and over again for the past three decades. Coin dealers have had so-called experts report on silver, gold, strategic metals, diamonds, colored gemstones, and rare or semi-rare coins. It is exactly the same thing the stock brokerages have done for years and for which they are finally being brought to task.

There are dealers who have reams of data on why rare coins are guaranteed to go up. The problem is, they haven't. Rare coins have been mostly down for over twenty years. But these dealers continue to tout the same facts year after year. Why? The answer is they sell rare coins and make a healthy profit on them. Every investor has no doubt seen the same thing with predictions of various rare coins.

The other day, a client sent me a list of coins he purchased from another dealer back in 1987 for $46,000. Included in the literature he sent was a projected price of $184,000. When I asked him about it, he told me a very well-known dealer published this price in a book.

Yet, twenty-three years later, the coins are worth $5,800. The projection was nothing more than a way to separate this investor from his money, even though the dealer may or may not have firmly believed what he said.

Be very cautious of these analysts. They write pamphlets and books that show one side of the argument. Ask yourself, if these coins were so rare and guaranteed to make such huge gains, why are they selling? Ask your broker how many he personally owns. Ask him how much money he personally has made buying the coins he recommends. You will find most of these brokers don't own coins and simply make money by selling them for a large commission. That's okay—it's their job.

But one broker told a client that his recommendations had gone up 1,200 % in one year! Yet, he couldn't provide references of clients who made these profits.

Another large broker claims that $20 St. Gaudens in MS-63 go up $3 for every $1 that gold goes up. That would mean they would have to be almost $5,000 each. The fact is, they are worth a fairly small premium of a few hundred dollars over gold. The reality is they have gone up about 70c for every $1 gold has gone up.

Many brokers/dealers make claims without checking to see if what they are saying is correct. This is especially true when they talk about confiscation. They will try to trade you out of Eagles and Buffaloes in favor of $20 gold Liberties and St. Gaudens. Yet, the Buffalo and Eagle gold coins are specifically defined in legislation as "numismatic" coins. Therefore, they are a much safer bet if you are worried about confiscation of gold.

There are many, many good dealers out there. Some are absolute geniuses when it comes to coin history. Beware of those who do nothing but promote the coins they sell. They are not necessarily dishonest, but they are blinded more by what they want to happen then what really does.

Remember the stock analysts and apply it to coin analysts. Then do research yourself before you spend your money. I believe it's only a matter of time before the regulators and lawyers look at the investment coin market the same way they do the stock market. Ironically, a bull market in rare coins (which is what everyone is waiting for) could easily be the catalyst. I see people weekly who have lost hundreds of thousands of dollars based solely on a broker's recommendations and those of so-called analysts. While many people say it will be a good thing to go after some of these dealers, the fact is it could completely cripple the already fragile coin market.

Some of the regulations may be reasonable and some even well meaning. The effect on the long-term prospects for this market is disastrous. It will be great for collectors, because it will no doubt force all but the most educated investors from the market. The unintended consequence of this further regulation will be even less guidance from your dealer. Dealers will not be able to shoulder the responsibility for your portfolio.

Many buyers didn't do their homework and blindly trusted dealers or brokers on the phone. "Buyer beware" seems to be a forgotten edict when the huge losses occur; instead, they run to lawyers and governments to blame the dealer.

If you decide to stay in or jump into the rare coin market, you will have to be more and more in touch with it. You will be required to stay current and become educated, because your dealer will not be able to do it for you.

CHAPTER 21
GOLD CONFISCATION

In my opinion, one of the biggest lies in the coin world is:

"You need to buy $20 St. Gaudens, $20 Liberties to protect yourself from government confiscation."

What's happened for years and years is that the dealers and telemarketers have used Franklin Roosevelt's executive order of 1933 to say, "There's a law on the books that allows the President to confiscate gold or regulate gold during times of national emergency." The argument is that because it's already on the books, it doesn't have to go through Congress. They claim the President can wake up tomorrow morning and say, "The terrorists are out there, and in the interest of national security, we're confiscating gold today." This is not exactly true. There are so many holes in their theory; I can't cover all of them in this book, but I'll give you the basics as I see them.

There's one thing that is certain: there is a confiscation you need to worry about—it's the dealers and brokers confiscating your money.

The truth is, some dealers actually think there's a chance it could happen. In other words, I don't think they believe they're lying, but they really are telling myths, not facts. It is more a question of them not doing their homework.

When gold was legalized in 1974, President Gerald Ford repealed this act. After all, how can you confiscate gold and make it legal to own at the same time?

The problem is, dealers will have a great scare tactic that allows them to sell highly profitable coins to investors. They'll take one piece of information and twist it and use it to their benefit. They seldom do their research. They never find out if what they're saying is true.

Here's the number one reason dealers love to use the confiscation issue: It's very emotional. It's very easy to scare you to death on the phone and claim the government is after you. Remember, people who are buying gold coins are very afraid of "Big Brother." Even if you buy into the notion that the law is still on the books (again, it's not), it's ridiculous to assume that twenty-dollar gold pieces these dealers are selling are nonconfiscatable and safe, especially in the lower grades like VF, XF, AU, and MS-60 to MS-63. These are the coins the government actually did confiscate.

First, we're going to assume the worst, which is the government wants to call in all of the gold. The Executive Order of 1933, that President Roosevelt issued, has one sentence in it that these dealers point to.

The order specifically says that all gold coins are confiscatable, "except Gold coins having recognized special value to collectors of rare and unusual coins."

From that statement, many of these dealers have somehow come up with the idea that any "collectible" coin is exempt; coins that have 15 percent% premiums are exempt or coins that are one hundred years old are exempt. In other words, they've added their own subjective ideas to this. But that's not what it says. It doesn't define "special value." It does not define who a collector is. It certainly doesn't tell you what a collectible is. And it doesn't tell you who decides this.

It's a loophole you could drive a truck through, but investors are assuming there's hard criteria that the government would have to follow.

Dealers are out there selling "nonconfiscatable" coins, typically, the twenty dollar gold pieces, the \$20 St. Gaudens, and the Liberties, based on this supposed loophole. They also sell a lot of other coins that they claim fall in this category. Understand that they include \$5, \$10, and \$2½ gold pieces, too.

Here's the comical part of this: most of the coins that these dealers are selling come from hoards in Europe. The hoards in Europe are coins that the U.S. government confiscated and sent to Europe to pay off debts. These coins are supposed to be nonconfiscatable, but the government actually confiscated those same coins in 1933 and then paid off foreigners with these supposedly nonconfiscatable coins. So, these dealers are selling you coins as nonconfiscatable, but in many cases, they're the actual coins that were confiscated!

You must remember that when the law was written, these were coins of the realm. These coins were used in everyday trade. When they confiscated gold, these $20 Liberties and $20 St. Gaudens, as well as the $5, $10, and $2 gold coins, were what they confiscated. So, no one can say that even though the government confiscated these coins the first time, they're now considered rare and unusual and can't be confiscated today. The government could overcome that very easily. They've got precedence on their side. We confiscated them once, so, of course, we can confiscate them again.

Let's take a look at it from another standpoint. Are these coins rare and unusual? PCGS and NGC are the two largest coin-grading services. They had graded more than 1,513,192 $20 St. Gaudens and more than 984,830 $20 Liberties by the beginning of 2010. These are mostly the higher-quality coins, because it's not profitable to pay the grading fees on low-grade coins, so there are many coins that are lower quality out there. They grade thousands of those coins every month.

The government actually minted 103,835,171 $20 Liberties and 69,833,846 $20 St. Gaudens. So, it's guaranteed that the population (number of coins graded) will continue to grow by leaps and bounds.

It's very easy to shoot a hole in the premise that those coins are rare and unusual. They're anything but rare and far from unusual.

The thing I want people to realize is this: even if you assume that this law is still on the books and the government may confiscate gold, buying the high-priced semi-numismatic coins does absolutely nothing to protect you from confiscation. In fact, they're the exact coins the government confiscated the first time. It gives you absolutely no protection.

The second item that I look at as far as confiscation goes is, assuming the law was on the books, would the government really even bother to confiscate gold? In 1933, they confiscated gold because everyone had gold in his or her pocket. There were gold certificates and gold coins. They were making the coins. That's what was used every day for commerce. They were even being used in the banks.

What I'm driving at is that confiscating gold affected almost everyone. Almost everyone had gold, so the government was able to take in millions and millions of ounces of gold. What would they gain today? Even if the government decided to confiscate gold, how much gold do you think people actually own in this country? I highly doubt if even 3 % of the U.S. public owns any physical gold bullion. It's simply a nonissue. For the amount of trouble the government would have to go through, it wouldn't be worth it. The people who own gold today (and when I say gold, I'm talking about any type of gold that's been sold as a hedge, whether it's European, U.S. gold coins, or even the modern bullion coins) have such a small physical amount that, even if the government got all of it, it's not going to amount to anything substantial in its eyes.

A few billion dollars is nothing to the government. The second problem they would have confiscating is that the people who own gold today, for the most part, own it specifically because they're afraid of the government. So, unless the government is going to go door to door with guns, these people are not going to voluntarily take that gold and turn it in. So again, assuming that the law is on the books, I think the chance of the government ever enforcing it is almost zero, as they have nothing to gain.

If you buy into the story that the government is out there, waiting to confiscate your gold, there's very little you can do to protect yourself from it. My conclusion …

> If anyone induced, persuaded, or outright scared you into buying rare coins to be protected from gold confiscation, that should not be a reason for you to hold onto your value-losing coins any longer.

CHAPTER 22
THE TAXMAN

The following is my understanding about tax consequences and policy. However, you should always consult with a tax professional versed in your own situation.

Coins and bullion are treated much the same as stocks when it comes to capital gains and losses.

If you have losses on coins or bullion, you can claim them against investment gains. That could save you a lot in taxes owed on a performing investment.

For example:

> You paid $25,000 for coins, which are now worth $10,000. That gives you a $15,000 loss. Suppose you have gains on some other investment you'd like to take, let's say a $15,000 gain on real estate or stocks. You offset your $15,000 loss against your $15,000 gain to create a tax-free situation for your gain. Depending on your tax bracket and on whether your gain was long term or short term, you just "made" an extra $3,000 to $5,000 or more. I've seen cases where the tax savings were more than sale price of the coins.

Even if you have no gains, you can carry the loss forward and deduct $3,000 a year from your income. This will produce up to another $1,200 tax savings, which is money in your pocket. At the time of this writing, they are talking about raising this deduction to $8,250 a year, which will put even more money in your pocket. Remember, you can carry this loss forward.

Tax Disadvantages

This reason for selling goes along with tax advantages but with a twist.

Many people state, "I'll just leave them to my kids or grandkids." They are hoping that time will make the investment pay off, even though they may have held it for twenty years already. Allow me to explain the sheer irony of what will happen if by some chance they are right.

First of all, the tax savings that could be had by taking the loss are completely lost when someone inherits or is given your coins. They are valued as of the day you die or give them away. You can flush the tax savings down the drain—they're gone. To add insult to injury, let's suppose a miracle happens and the coins actually go up to the original price paid. The "gain" is then taxable. That's right, even though the original price might have been, let's say, $100,000 on the coins and they were valued at $25,000 when inherited and then went back up to $100,000 in value, there will be taxes owed on the $75,000 "gain" to your heirs. It actually costs them to break even.

Some people will think, "Who's going to know?" I guess that's true if you don't mind risking tax evasion or fraud. For the rest of us, the tax advantages or penalties make these factors very important.

Read the chapter on Regulations. I believe it is naïve to believe that rare coins will remain the "private" investment it has been for decades. The Patriot Act and other security regulations are substantially altering this market. I suspect in the next three to five years, there will be fewer dealers and significantly increased regulation of money coming and going in the coin market.

SECTION V

TIME FOR A CHANGE: TRADE OR SELL YOUR RARE COINS

CHAPTER 23
WHAT TO DO IF YOU ALREADY OWN COINS

The first thing you need to do is find out where you stand.

Do you really know what your coins are worth? Or, are you guessing and hoping what the value may be? When gold goes up, do you simply assume your coins are keeping pace? If they do, how will you know?

How and where do you start?

American Federal provides a performance review that will show you exactly how your coins have performed in comparison to gold or silver. Call 800-221-7694 for this information.

If the dealer you bought from is still in business, give them a call. This will be a test for both of you. The dealer will probably tell you their perception of the market during this call. Beware if all the dealer wants to do is talk you into holding longer and avoids giving you pricing information. Tell your dealer that you want to know the liquidation value of your coins. You need this so you can make some informed decisions. This should not take your dealer very long to do, although it can take a few days if you're dealing with a broker or salesperson, because he or she will have to get the prices from someone else. But certainly, there's no excuse for it to take more than a week, unless you have a very complicated portfolio—which is rare—or if your dealer travels frequently and is out of the office.

When you get the liquid value of your coins, it's time to take an honest look at what you bought.

Reexamine the reason you bought coins. Do you know why you bought? Were you afraid of Y2K, inflation, war, deflation, government policies, and so on? Did you do it as an investment? Or did a dealer, broker, or salesperson talk you into it? If you had a real reason for buying, does it still apply? Many people bought as a hedge for Y2K. Yet, Y2K came and went, and most people continue to hold their coins. It's like keeping your auto insurance after you've stopped driving and sold your car.

Was it a hedge for the inflation that really never returned from the 1970s? Do you believe inflation is still a potential problem? Have your coins really protected you so far? If not, why waste more time holding for a problem that's come and gone? People have a way of fearing those bad times. It's healthy to be aware and not be a Pollyanna. At the same time, I see many people do nothing but plan for the bad times. They never plan for or enjoy the good times. There needs to be a balance.

Look at the last one hundred years. How few of them were actually terrible times? Perhaps only ten to fifteen years. Why waste decades of good times, making no money and usually losing a substantial amount of money, to plan only for a couple bad years? Do the concerns that made you buy coins still apply? Would you have been better off not buying coins?

The answers to these questions should help tell you what to do with what you own. Maybe you should get out or at least lighten your position. If you still have concerns, maybe bullion would better serve your purpose.

Even if your concerns have not changed, or if you perceive the same problems persisting for the last thirty, twenty, or ten years, ask yourself honestly, "Have the coins you owned really served any purpose? Have they really, truly been a hedge?" If not, what's going to change to make the coins profitable, or to at least serve as the hedge you thought you bought?

It's unfortunate, but for most people, the coins they bought as a hedge against tragedy and collapse have turned into their own tragedy. It's ironic that "the hedge" has instead turned into "the problem" for many people.

I met a lady who owned coins she had purchased with a credit card. She believed what a high-pressure salesman had told her. She envisioned doubling her money, paying off the credit card, and pocketing the profit.

After a year and a half, her broker stopped calling her when she stopped buying. Her calls eventually went unanswered when she inquired about the liquidation value of coins. She had coins, debt, and no one to talk to.

After we talked, I told her, "I can guarantee you at least 21 % on your coins." She was beside herself. How could I do that?

It's easy: you simply sell the coins for what they're worth. I can do that for you. Then you save the 21 % and you pay your credit card. She did it. Needless to say, she did not recoup what she paid; she got about half. But she stopped paying most of the interest on a non-appreciating investment and was able to finally pay off her credit cards.

If you still feel you need a hedge or investment, find a good, honest dealer. There are a lot of them out there. Evaluate how yours has performed thus far, and see if that dealer can suggest a way to answer your concerns by repositioning into truly rare coins, bullion, or by cashing out. Depending on your particular situation, maybe something safer or with less volatility is the way for you to go. Or, you might just cash out to pay off bills or invest elsewhere.

CHAPTER 24
BITING THE BULLET

Benefits of Selling

The single most beneficial aspect of selling coins is the mental freedom that comes with unloading a losing investment. Or, if you're one of the few in profit, it may be a great idea to lock it in and sell while you're a winner.

Literally hundreds of people have told me how they felt "a weight had been lifted" from their shoulders afterward. Of course, it is often traumatic until the decision is made. Why is selling liberating?

There are many reasons. First, it's nice to not have to think about it anymore. I can tell you firsthand about that feeling. I jumped into the stock market with both feet in 1999. In hindsight, it was not such a great time. For a while, it looked like I was a genius. I had a predetermined goal of how much I wanted to make and how much I'd risk (this may sound like your coin-buying experience). It didn't take long for me to have my "risk" capital invested several times. The broker always had another great deal that I just had to get in on.

It all sounded so great. Of course, I really didn't know anything about stocks, so I kept taking the broker's word for it. I assumed he must know what he's doing; after all, he had lots of clients.

Well, all of a sudden the market did a huge about-face. I remember seeing my portfolio drop six figures in a week! So yes, I can empathize with many coin buyers. I was very nervous and quite irritable. Instead of taking my losses and moving on, the broker convinced me to stick it out. After all, how bad could it get?

I stuck with it against my better judgment. When it first went down, I'd say, "If I can just break even, I'll get out." Then there was a rally that got me back to even. But I got greedy and didn't get out. The market dropped again, and I was saying, "Well, if I can only lose 50 %, I'll get out." I finally got out after losing 80 %. It gnawed at me for months. I'm not dumb, so how did I lose so much money?

Not only did I not realize my goal (and I could've early in the game), but I lost five times what I thought I had risked! Eventually, I got over the shame, the shock, and the horror of what I'd done. Now I'm not bothered or anxious about whether the stock market goes up or down every day. Invariably, I'm happy I got out because many of my so-called sure bets dropped another 80 % or more. In fact, I sold one stock at $150 and then bought back at $100. Eventually I bailed out at $48, and it is now $2.93! I also made some money back in areas I knew more about. I'm just glad it's over.

What's the point of my story? My foray into stocks, an area I knew nothing about, was similar to many people's experience in coins. If I had cut my losses the minute I knew I had made a mistake, I'd have been much better off financially, as well as mentally. Instead of my moods being influenced every day by my family, it was influenced by a mindset over which I had no control. It was a horrible year, filled with tension and heartbreak but still a valuable lesson. It emphasized something I've heard for years but never figured out until now: your first loss is your best loss.

Tax Advantages

The second reason may or may not apply to your particular case, but it is extremely important. If you have a loss on your coins or bullion, you can most likely claim it on your income taxes.

Let's be clear about one thing. I do not recommend you take gains or losses solely for tax reasons, but if you can obtain some gain (by taking a loss), it should help. I'm not an accountant, but I believe what I'm stating here is correct. I know hundreds of clients who have done this with no problems, but check with your own accountant first. Everyone's situation is unique. We'll explore this more in another chapter.

Eat, Drink, and Be Merry, for Tomorrow …

The third benefit of selling is the most obvious: use the money for either investing or just enjoyment.

Personally, I'd rather enjoy some spare cash if it's money you don't really need. In our business, we see lots of people between the ages of seventy and ninety-five. Many people tell me they'd like to travel, help their kids, send their grandkids to college, or simply spend the money on themselves.

I had one client sell and then go out and buy a motor home the next day. She said that if she's going to tie up her money in a depreciating asset, she might as well enjoy it while she can. I don't mean to minimize anyone's loss, but there is a lot of truth in her outlook. Many people will tell me, "I'm not going to sell because I don't need the money." Sometimes need and want are different, so why not spend it on yourself? Or, spend it on a loved one and watch them enjoy it instead of waiting to inherit it. Or, invest it in something safer.

It may sound wanton to tell you to spend your own money. If the bulk of coin investors I see and talk to were getting rich or even keeping slightly ahead of the game, I'd be recommending investing in coins.

To some people, the idea of spending the money just to spend it won't sit well. Then, why not invest somewhere safe with a real return? At the end of the year, you'll see an increase; even if it's a small gain, it's better than a constant loss. "I can't settle for 2 % or 3 % a year on my money," is something I hear constantly.

However, it's very rare that I find a coin investor who has actually made 2 % a year over the last twenty years.

Finally, keep in mind the reason you bought coins, usually as an investment or hedge, not as an heirloom. If you indeed did buy as a true collector, please continue. Most of this does not apply to you. For the other 98 % of the readers, please keep your goals in mind.

When your dealer says, "Coins will be a great heirloom," what he is really saying is, "You bought an overpriced, hyped coin that's going nowhere."

Do you really want to leave your losses, your mistakes, to your heirs? I know that I don't. I want to leave them winning, so they remember how smart I was. Many people have done really well in investments in general but have a tough time accepting their losses in coins. In fact, most coin investors I meet are extremely smart individuals, who have done much better than the average investor. That's why they had the money to diversify into coins in the first place. Not every investment works out though. If this one hasn't, it's time to do something about it.

If you are one of the few who either have a great dealer or a lot of personal knowledge and time invested, stick with it.

If you believe you still need the protection you initially sought, you should consider selling your coins and putting the money in gold bullion like Eagles, Krugerrands, or similar bullion type coins, if the coins are not achieving your goals.

CHAPTER 25
There Are Seven Places to Sell Your Coins: Proceed at Your Own Risk

1. **The Internet**
   Many people use Craigslist and e-Bay to sell everything from used shoes to multi-million dollar mansions. It takes a certain quality to do this with coins. You must be willing to set up an account, answer questions, ship to various buyers, and worry about getting paid. It's a lot of work. People, including other dealers who have done this, have told me it's a real hassle, not to mention time consuming. In addition, if you really don't know the market very well, you may be in over your head. Let's face it ... a lot of people are losing money because they were taken advantage of because of their limited knowledge in the first place. You are also reaching buyers who want a deal. My experience with auctions is that unless you have something super spectacular, most people attending (or buying online) are looking for a deal. Isn't that why so many people shop the Internet? It's cheaper. Even after all this, you'll still have to pay a fee and/or commission.

2. **Small Coin Shops**
   I can't say anything categorically about small shops. Some are great, and some are horror houses. I'm always concerned about guys who run a shop just because gold is hot. Since gold took off, it seems like everyone is a gold or coin "expert." If you look to local shops, you must realize that unless they are very involved nationally and attend major auctions and shows, they may be in their own little market. They will be at the whim of whatever the local collectors are into, not necessarily what's going on in the broader market. I hear complaints that, "a local dealer paid half of what it was worth." Some people feel ripped off if this happens. But remember, the local dealer may keep all he buys and tries to sell retail through the store location. If he buys coins from you, coins he doesn't specialize in, they could sit for a year

before the right buyer shows up. So realistically, he has to double his money to make a decent return. I think the local dealer is much better than a pawnshop, jewelry store, or collectibles store. They probably pay several times what the hotel buyers pay.

3. **Pawnshops**
   Pawnshops, part-time or general collectibles stores, and places like barbershops that happen to have signs that say, "We Buy Gold," are fine if you just have to have cash that minute, but generally these places are going to pay very low rates. These guys are part-time coins guys at best. They need to be extra safe (cheap), because many don't really know the market, but if they buy it cheap enough, it doesn't matter. I had a pawnshop owner call me years ago to buy out his coin accumulation. He thought he knew what he was doing, but it was incredible. He had polished counterfeits, priced in the thousands of dollars. When I pointed it out, he didn't care. He said he only paid a third of the gold price and would sell them as MS-63s or MS-65s to people who came in. We were not able to do business.

4. **Hotel Buyers**
   The hotel buyers seem to show up every time the market gets hot. They need to spend a lot of money and get a high return. I believe a lot of them pay as little as twenty-five cents on the dollar. They run full-page ads with incredible prices. Usually it says "up to" price, meaning you won't get it. They want you to think it's like the TV show *Antiques Roadshow*. It's not. In the past, I've talked with some of these guys. They love telling stories about the great deals they got. One guy told me he bought what someone thought was a roll of Indian cents, valued at around $50, but they really were $2½ Indian gold coins worth about $10,000.00. I'm not saying they are a bunch of crooks, but I think they come in for a weekend, looking to make great buys. And if anyone wants to complain, they are in a new town a week later.

In a recent article in *Coin Dealer Newsletter* the executive director of PNG says that traveling hotel buyers offer only pennies on the dollar. One such dealer offered only $60 for a rare $2½ Indian in MS-66, which has a bid of $8,500!

American Federal does travel to clients' homes, businesses, and banks to buy coins. We are not a hotel buyer, who flies in and out of town after town with full-page ads. We are a specialized coin buyer with a long history and references.

The average hotel coin buyer has gone into business just to take advantage of the current market boom and prey on uneducated sellers.

5. **Gold Parties**
   I'm not a fan a gold parties either. How do you know who is buying what? If you just think about it, it's a step down from the hotel guys.

6. **Gold Mail-Ins**
   Next are the guys who just want you to mail your gold in and get an offer. I wouldn't mail anything without something in writing as to what I'm getting. If it's scrap gold, I want to know how much per gram or karat I'm getting. If it's rare coins, I want a written offer. This goes for sending coins to national dealers or even the dealer from whom you bought them. Many dealers will send you an offer good only the day they mailed it. Wow! How exactly do you take advantage of that? Or, they say it's an indication, but after they get your coins, they'll tell you what they'll pay. Others claim that the prices change hourly or more, so you just have to trust them. They never tell you what you can actually expect. If they intend to pay you, they should have no problem guaranteeing a price in writing. I've seen too many people send coins, expecting one price only to get less or worse yet, overpriced coins in return.

7. **Large National Dealer**

The best dealer, in my biased opinion (because I am one) is a large national dealer. We physically deal in all fifty states; we deal with market makers, auctioneers, and both collectors and their representatives. Believe it or not, only a handful of dealers do most of the business.

I'm not saying anything about the small dealer or the guy who's a one-man show, working out of his house, but it takes a lot of manpower and relationships to stay on top of things. Getting the *Coin Dealer Newsletter* is a step almost every dealer takes. As national dealers, we need to know who is behind the bids. Why they are buying tells a whole different story. If someone is buying simply to support inventory, it's different than someone buying in anticipation of doing a major promotion.

Look at these examples. Let's suppose a dealer has 500 MS-65 $20 St. Gaudens in stock. He is also the high bidder on MS-65 Saints. That's a red flag for me. Is he really trying to buy more or just trying to keep the list price up while he gets rid of his inventory? On the other hand, other dealers may be stockpiling certain coins and hiring brokers or sending direct mail or e-mail to promote a new area of the market. (See my chapter, "How to Use Dealer Promos to Profit").

These dealers should be members of national coin industry organizations. The best is PNG, the Professional Numismatic Guild.

CHAPTER 26
TO WHOM DO I SELL?

First, you think that going back to the dealer who sold the coins to you would be the way to go. In many cases, that is a good place to start.

But don't be surprised to find your dealer doesn't buy back. A quick visit to various Web sites turned up a lot of disclaimers. As of this writing:

- Universal Coin and Bullion says they charge a 20 % restocking fee for returned coins.
- Lear Financial says they don't guarantee to buy back and further warns that prices change hourly or more.
- Goldline also says they can't legally promise to buy back, and they say they have a 30 to 35 % markup on coins like Swiss 20 Francs (a bullion coin!).
- Merit Financial recommends a holding period of five to ten years to cover spreads.
- Blanchard also does not guarantee to repurchase.

This does not mean any of these companies are doing anything unethical or wrong. Just the opposite: they are honest enough to tell you the truth if you just look for it. It just means your rare coins really may not be as liquid as you may believe.

What happens if you decide to sell when no one really wants to buy?

Bullion coins offer much greater liquidity. While I certainly agree that no one can guarantee there will be a market to resell your coins, you can greatly shift the odds in your favor by buying or trading into bullion coins like American Gold and Silver Eagles or Gold Buffaloes.

If you feel you were overcharged, taken advantage of, and

harassed by your dealer, I would suggest not going back for more.

I've had clients who had paid prices 70 % to 200 % over current market decide they were going to force or trick their dealer into buying back the coins. That is a terrible idea. They do not have to buy your coins. In fact, there are times when your coins simply are not liquid.

Second, many of the large dealers are set up to sell coins to you, not buy them back. Your broker doesn't get paid to buy back unless he can trade you into something on which they can make another profit.

One client didn't believe me. He decided that since he overpaid for his coins because of his negligence to check prices, he would be smarter the second time around. He shopped and shopped. Finally, a dealer out of New York gave him an unbelievable offer, several times what I was able to offer. Well, he thought his hard work paid off. Eventually, he received coins back in trade from the dealer, not a check and not bullion, of which he would have known the value.

They sold him coins at what appeared to be reasonable prices. The problem was that they delivered NCS coins, not NGC coins. The grade of the coins was so terrible I almost choked! One coin he paid $20,000 for was graded MS-63 by the company. In reality, the coin was barely XF-45 and worth $1,000. So the story went, his entire portfolio, about $105,000 from what I saw, was really now worth less than $6,000.

You are not going to get the better of a dealer. They are at this full time. They know what's going on. They are experts, albeit some are crooked ones.

So, call your dealer if you were happy with them and feel you were treated fairly. Ask for an offer in writing, have them fax it, mail it, or e-mail it. It should be good for a certain amount of time.

Sometimes the bid is good only for the day it is given. That doesn't do you any good if they mail the offer. If that's the case, it tells you they are not really giving you an offer. If the price is good for one day only, they should fax it or e-mail it and give you a chance to accept it.

If any of these things happen, you should stop trying to sell back. They don't want your coins.

- It takes weeks to give you an offer – get another dealer.
- They won't give you an offer in writing – get another dealer.
- They don't want to fax or e-mail it –get another dealer.
- They won't guarantee the price –get another dealer.
- They will only trade –get another dealer.
- They need a few days to count the coins – get another dealer.
- They stop returning your calls – get another dealer.
- They want you to just ship your coins – get another dealer.
- They want you to buy another coin or two to finish the set first – get another dealer.

These are all warning signs. They scream, "We don't want to buy your coins!" They may quote you one price only to pay you another; it happens all the time. They may quote you a price and then deliver other coins in return for all or part of the transaction.

It's this easy… If they are going to buy your coins, they should be just as anxious to talk to you as when they sold coins to you. Pay attention to these warning signs. Don't try to outmaneuver the dealer or let your hope cloud your judgment.

SECTION VI

HOW TO REPOSITION FOR A SIMPLER FUTURE

CHAPTER 27
YOU'VE DECIDED TO SELL, NOW GET EVERY DOLLAR!

After looking at how most rare coins have performed in comparison to gold, you probably need to figure out how to sell your coins, and you likely want every penny you can get.

Almost all dealers tell you they will buy back your coins when you are ready to sell. The reality is the bulk of them would rather shoot themselves in the knee than buy your rare coins for cash.

Do yourself a favor. Don't think you're going to make your dealer buy them, get the better of him in a trade, or trick him to get your money back. I've seen hundreds of people try to, "teach their dealers a lesson," or make them honor what they said. It won't work. They know the market—you don't. You will never beat them at their own game. In fact, you are more likely to end up even further behind.

One client of mine was so determined to get every dollar out of his coins, he decided he would simply find the "right dealer" to buy his coins and save my commission charge. He just didn't understand the market.

The fact is that it's extremely rare that one dealer can pay you 50 %, 100 %, or 300 % more than another dealer. Sure, it happens on super rarities on occasion, but not on regularly traded coins.

He called me, his dealer, and a fly-by-night New York dealer to get "bids". His dealer's bid was almost 20 % higher than mine, so on the first transaction, he sent the coins back to the dealer, who took advantage of him in the first place. I tried to convince him that just because he bought coins from this dealer didn't mean they were obligated to pay more. He sent his coins back without getting a firm offer in writing.

I always tell people to get it in writing. It can be a fax, handwritten note, or e-mail, but it should be a firm guarantee, in writing, on company letterhead or an invoice. And, it should include a statement that tells when you can expect payment in full by check or wire, not trade! (Be cautious about a value statement that indicates the offer is good for only the day made, usually five days before you could receive it in the mail.) What he received, two months later, was a check for half of the quoted amount and a group of $10 Indian Gold coins for the balance. He thought he did good, until he found out the Indian Gold coins were priced at close to double the current bid.

Then, since he thought he finally learned his lesson, he asked again for the offer in writing. The request was made. Then "lost" in the mail. When finally received, it again disclaimed any bid that was supposedly made. In addition, the offer made for MS-70 Buffalo First Strikes was only about $50 over spot, which proves there is no market for these coins.

So, with this batch of coins, he tried again. This time, he tried a new dealer. This dealer was offering prices much higher than mine or his dealer. Again, he shipped his coins. This time, he got $10 Indians again, only they were graded by a totally worthless, unrecognized grading service—not NGC, PCGS, or ANACS (the only ones worth having, in my opinion).

I visited him again to see how he was doing. I believe he thought he really had found a way out of his predicament. The coins were both grossly overgraded and overpriced. The total liquid value, before any commission or profit for me, was $5,025. He paid $60,000 for one coin alone, which I valued at $750. When I looked at his invoice, he had paid $99,700 for coins worth less than $6,000.

The sad part of the story is that by not doing any work other than taking a broker's word over the phone when he bought coins, he gave up a lot of money right off the bat. Then—in an effort to make up for it, he decided to, "get every last dollar for the rest," by saving a commission and thinking he could do it all himself—he really lost money. When I first met this gentleman, he had approximately $350,000 worth of coins. By the time he traded and outsmarted the dealers, he had about $37,000 left.

You need to realize that no dealer is going to buy your coins and make nothing. Some claim there is no commission or profit when you sell. That is rarely the case. Although if it's true, it explains why the minute you tell them you want to sell, they stop returning calls.

Anyone you sell to is going to make money on your coins. That's what they are in business to do. If you think you can get on the phone and find the guy paying way over market for your coins, you are fooling yourself and likely looking for a larger loss. There are always exceptions. If you have truly super rare coins, a knowledgeable dealer may get you over market if he knows exactly who to sell to. But, if you bought from a broker or over the phone, you are not likely to have this type of coins.

The problem is that too many people believed a broker about how great coins were, how he would get you the best, or a great story of how you would make money on some great deal the dealer had that day. Many people simply took their dealer's word for it and sent a check without verifying what the coins were worth.

I just visited a lady who spent $497,000 with one of the radio talk show recommended dealers. Thirty days later, when she decided she made a mistake, they offered her $300,000. That an almost $200,000 loss (40 %) in one month! (By the way, neither gold nor her coins had gone down in that time.) Then, to add insult to injury, they would not guarantee to pay that price even when she offered to drive the coins to Los Angeles and deliver them.

It's impossible to make that loss up when you sell the coins, yet that's what so many people try to do.

They tell me they need to get every last dollar out of their coins. They are determined not to make the same mistake twice. But they do by chasing false, unrealistic bids that dealers have no intention of paying. If you have hundreds of thousands of dollars worth of coins, your dealer should be happy to hop on a plane and pick them up.

Even if this lady found someone willing to sell these coins as a favor and make nothing, she still couldn't come anywhere close to breaking even. Don't expect to make up for exorbitant markups by trying to make it up on the sale of your coins. You can't, and it's likely to put you in worse shape, or you are promised more and end up with less.

Another consequence of overshopping your coins when you sell is that you may inadvertently lower the price of your own coins. Many people don't believe me, but when you call five to ten dealers, they each call several more. If you have somewhat rare coins or ones of any decent quantity, you can hurt your own price. There are really only a handful of people who will end up with your coins.

I had a gentleman call around trying to sell 100 MS-66 $20 St. Gaudens. I warned him to be careful, but I think he was convinced I just didn't want him getting other bids, so he called many dealers. So many dealers, that I was offered the coins by another dealer, and three other dealers I know had also heard about the coins. What happened was that no one knew for sure if there were one hundred or five hundred coins out there. When that happens, dealers get scared and the bids dropped ... in this case, over 11 %.

The best thing to do is talk to a dealer with whom you're comfortable. Ask him what current *Coin Dealer Newsletter* is if you want an easy reference for pricing. Let one dealer handle the sale at an agreed-upon commission or fee and then let him do the job. Make sure it's a cash offer, or if you are not ready to exit the market, trade for bullion or bullion-type coins that move with the price of gold or silver and are only a small amount over the daily price of gold.

If the dealer you talk to won't make a cash offer in writing, don't send your coins. If he wants to trade for graded bullion coins or other rare coins, don't send your coins. If he avoids your calls, won't call back, doesn't give prices in a timely manner, or tells you the big move is coming any day now, go elsewhere. This business does not want to buy your coins. The more you push the issue, the worse it will get.

Find someone, like my company, American Federal, 1-800-221-7694, who will tell you what your coins are worth and how much they will guarantee to pay you.

Many people are in a loss situation, because they really didn't know the coin market well enough when they bought. If they haven't become coin experts since they (or you) bought the coins, they need to leave the selling to someone who is an expert. Buying something they knew little about is what caused the problem, and it will create another problem when selling as your own representative.

CHAPTER 28
YOU'VE DECIDED TO SELL: USE CAUTION

Go it alone? Go with an adviser?

How Do You Do It?

You have several options.

Do It Yourself

You can (but I wouldn't recommend it) go it alone by placing an ad in your local newspaper.

You see this all the time—local collector has silver dollars or miscellaneous gold coins or what have you. For some people and true collectors, they have a ball with these, because they love having other collectors go through and look at their coins and pick and choose. It's a whole social event, and they have a great time.

Most of the people reading this book are probably not in that category. For most people, it means having people you don't know come to your house. And you have no way to tell if they are knowledgeable about coins. Chances are, if you bought from a telemarketer, you don't know a whole lot about coins yourself.

So, you're back in a position of having someone who may or may not know a lot more than you do showing up at your door. You're also putting yourself at risk. Let me tell you a true story that happened near my home.

There was a gentleman who lived not far from me in a very nice part of town. He had a half-million-dollar motor home. He listed it for sale in the paper. Someone called and showed up to look at his RV. He was then shot, and his motor home was stolen.

I'm not making this point to instill fear. I'm trying to caution you. If you want to sell your coins yourself, you can do it. But truthfully speaking, it may cost you more than the 10 to 20 % you save. If you do it yourself, you might not save at all.

That said, some people prefer doing it themselves. For those of you who do sell them yourself, here are some cautionary steps you should take. Never let strangers come to your house. Make sure they are qualified first. Unless you thoroughly check references, meet potential buyers in a neutral, protected place: your bank, your attorney's office, your accountant's office, or a public place like a restaurant.

You should be very careful whom you invite to your home. We meet lots of people at the bank. The banks don't mind having someone come in and look at your safe deposit box once or twice. But don't think you're going to go to the bank and tie up one of their rooms to show coins all day long, person after person. Unless you have a heck of a good relationship with your banker, it's not going to happen. If you use your lawyer's office, there may have a fee.

I have two friends who are what we call "Vest Pocket" dealers. In other words, they don't have stores. What they do is buy coins and then they'll try to resell from shop to shop. They'll sell a couple of coins here and there, and that's how they make a living. Just a few here and a few there, but they add up. They open their coat and there's a coin. One of the main ways they buy coins is by going to houses of people who have run ads in the paper, and they make them an offer for the whole collection. They generally buy the coins for 30 to 50 % less than I would pay for them.

So, unless you really, really know what you're doing, you really know your coins, you really know grading, and you really have a secure place to meet, it can be really dangerous—dangerous and unprofitable.

Auctions

The second way to sell is to consign your coins to an auction house to sell. If you decide to do this, use only one of the large auctioneers that specialize in coins. Any of the major coin auctioneers are very reputable.

Be aware, however, that the quality and rarity of the coins to be auctioned need to be good enough that the auction house wants to sell them. They need to be truly unusually rare or the collection to be very complete or unique. If you have the right coins, auctions may be the way to go.

Unless you have spectacular coins, you're probably going to end up paying anywhere from 10 to 20 %, depending on the deal you work out, which is a reasonable commission. You're going to have very little control over who gets to see your coins or the timing, because you generally have to consign your coins months in advance. So, you never know; the sale may hit at the worst possible time in the market or conversely, at the best.

Can you pull out of the auction? Sure you can, but usually for a fee. Either way, the auction house usually wants their commission. So, you could buy back your coins, but you're also going to pay something extra to buy them back. They're not going to do it for free, and it shouldn't be expected to.

The other thing that's not supposed to happen but does, is that many times, the catalogs are not going to people who want the coins. Just because it's an auction doesn't mean you're going to get the best price.

Why do you think so many people go to foreclosure auctions? Do you think they go because they're paying the highest price? They're going because they're getting a bargain. The same is true of many of the coin auctions. Every now and then, people read, "Oh, this coin brought in an unbelievable sum at auction or set a new record." That's usually the coin that is ultra rare or possibly under graded. Maybe the owner who put it in auction didn't really realize how nice the coin was, but that's the exception.

In my experience, unless you have really prime coins, there's no advantage to auctioning. Dealers attend most of the auctions and make most of the trades at auctions, and dealers don't buy at a disadvantage so they can lose money on the next sale.

In general, you're not always getting the retail buyer at the auction. I've been to many, many auctions, and it's the dealers who buy 90 % of the material. They're not paying retail. That's not necessarily bad, but you're not always getting as much money as you could unless your coins are spectacular.

You also have to beware of "collusion," although it's illegal. It works like this: there will be three dealers who get together and one will ask, "Which coins are you bidding on?"

"I'm bidding on these ten."

"I was going to bid on those ten, also."

"Well, let's write down our bids and see what each of us is willing to pay."

In this scenario, one dealer will say, "I was willing to pay three thousand." The next one says, "I was going to pay thirty-five hundred." The third says, "I was willing to pay thirty-four hundred." So, the two guys who were paying the least amount say, "Well, we won't bid on that and then you'll get it for less money." "Okay, but in return, you don't bid on this coin."

Again, there are things that are really, really out of your control. And I'm not casting any dispersion on the auction companies, because from my experience, the major auction companies are very good, very reputable, and beyond reproach. It's just that you have no control over anything. In fact, the Professional Numismatists Guild sent a letter to all its members warning them against "collusion" or "bid pooling." The letter also stated that this practice is illegal and a felony. But please beware: it still happens.

In some cases, I've heard people get 110 % of the hammer price, which sounds great. 10 % more than the auction price! Obviously, the auction company is not going to lose money. It just means the buyer is paying a higher commission. Either way, the commission is figured into the final price someone pays.

Coin Dealer Newsletter reported that the prices realized in several auctions were considerably less than wholesale bid. In fact, there was a good cross-section of coins that sold for 20 to 72 % below Bid. This happened in a so-called hot market!

That tells you that someone got a great deal by purchasing coins at under attended or under promoted auctions. The buyer—probably a dealer—was able to turn around and pocket a quick 20 to 70 % or more at the seller's expense.

The incredible thing about this is it did not happen in a poor market or at an obscure auction.

Sometimes, auctions don't bring enough competition to boost prices to ultra high levels unless the coins are classic rarities.

I handled an early, somewhat esoteric coin for a client. The buyer made me promise not to divulge which coin or its exact selling price, although I can tell you it was a six-figure coin.

By finding the right buyer, we were able to get more than double the last price paid at auction.

Why did we get such a good price? Could he have done better at auction?

Through long-established connections I had in the market, we were able to find the collector who truly wanted the coin. The coin was not presented as a sure sale, which is what an auction implies, although you can certainly place a minimum bid on most items.

The buyer knew that if we didn't get the "right price," his chance to purchase could disappear. So, he paid what it was really worth to him. Had this been an auction, it may have been very hard to duplicate those results … but we'll never know.

What are the chances two or more collectors would be willing to pay double for this coin? Would any sane dealer pay a substantial premium to stock the coin for inventory? I doubt it.

Even if my buyer showed up at auction, I doubt anyone would have bid against him at the higher prices. I believe that it would have likely sold for well below what we were able to get, but which he gladly paid.

At auction, we would have lost our leverage to hold out for more money unless someone bid against the buyer. We would have had little control on setting the price. Without another serious buyer, we would've likely had to depend on dealers to bid up the price, and I doubt they would've done that to the extent we wanted.

Instead, we regained control of the coin until the price was right.

For more discussion about auctions, please see "Frequently Asked Questions" at the back of this book.

Swap Meets

I've talked to people who took their coins to the local swap meet.

I personally think that's crazy, because you don't know who's at swap meets. If you have any kind of sizable number of coins or any value in your coins, you're not going to want to take $10,000 or $20,000 worth of coins to a swap meet. Swap meet or garage sales make sense to me if you have a hundred silver dollars or something like that. Just old worn-out silver dollars that are worth $10 to $16, and you're going to put them out for $25 each and really enjoy it. By all means then, go to the swap meet or have a garage sale.

You might sell eight coins for a lot of money at a swap meet. But people at the swap meets don't generally carry around thousands and thousands of dollars in cash. I don't know about you, but I'm not going to take somebody's check at a swap meet.

The Original Dealer

While you would think this is the best option, it often is not.

Most marketers make a one-way market—they *sell* coins. The broker/adviser does not get paid to buy back coins. As you can imagine, this drastically reduces the service you can expect. Selling dealers will often tell you there is no commission when you sell back to them. This is your first clue they really don't want to buy your coins. These dealers will often hide fees or offer to auction your coins. This takes the pricing out of their hands.

Common sense would indicate that if your dealer is a mass seller of rare coins, he should be anxious to buy your coins. Unfortunately, you will find it just isn't that way.

A company can have twenty, thirty, or even one hundred brokers selling coins, yet only one person who can price and buy coins to repurchase from you. Again, if they were interested in buying from you, they would certainly allocate more resources to this area. There are many reasons your original dealer may not be the best place to sell your coins.

First of all, they are set up to sell to you, not buy from you. The broker you have is likely not qualified to tell you what your coins are worth, much less offer to buy them. Your first clue is if you ask him what you could get for your coins, he will not quote your prices;

he will talk about why you shouldn't sell and finally tell you it may take a week to get prices. It's not his fault; he just is not authorized to buy, nor does he have any incentive to buy because he gets no commission on the purchase (unless he can trade you into other coins he can mark up and hide the "commission" in).

Second, if you are dealing with the dealer who may be driving a promotion or sector of the market, he simply can't buy back unless he has clients waiting. Frequently, a dealer will "become the market" for coins. For example, if Dealer F has promoted $2½ Indians for years, other dealers will look at what *he* pays when figuring their bids for $2½ Indians. If Dealer F suddenly shows up at a show with $2½ Indians for sale, the market could panic and prices could fall drastically, or the market could simply go into limbo (no longer buying or selling) until some other dealer decides to put up new bids. After all, if Dealer F has been the driving force behind $2½ Indians and suddenly goes from buying in the market to selling back into the market, a great amount of anxiety and caution and price discounting will follow, as dealers worry about what it means to the $2½ Indian market. If would be like Warren Buffet selling shares of Berkshire Hathaway!

Third is a relationship about which most "retail" buyers are unaware. There are often agreements made between the retail seller or dealer and his supplier. It's not unusual for a dealer to have an exclusive buying agreement with one or a couple of suppliers, so they are on the hook to buy from specific dealers. It's crazy, but sometimes the only way to sell to some of the larger dealers is to go through their designated supplier. Their supplier typically posts bids and buys coins specifically for them. This also explains why you can't get the best price when buying from these dealers.

I can tell you that dealing with the maze of buybacks, purchase requirements, and so on, can be mind-numbing, but it certainly affects a dealers' ability to buy from clients and even other dealers.

If you want to try your original dealer, do this:

1. Call and ask what you would receive in cash (check) for your coins. You don't want a trade you want money.
2. You will likely be told it will take a while to get prices. Ask how long. One week is certainly more than enough time.
3. If they actually call and give you prices in the quoted time frame, decide immediately if they are acceptable. If they are, ask them to put it in writing and include how much you will "net" and when you will get paid.

Some dealers will do all of this with no problem. It's the normal way to do business.

CAUTION: If your dealer will not perform in a timely manner (one week), put the offer in writing (standard business practice), and tell you when you get paid (common sense), you don't have a deal!

No matter how great they make it sound, they have no intention of buying your coins. Do not assume you have real prices. Do not deal with this person. Find a new dealer!

Some dealers will make it *appear* they are giving you a bid. When you read the fine print, it often says the bid is good for that day only. This is a problem if it's been in the mail for two or three days.

Can you imagine yourself sitting before a judge and telling him, "But Your Honor, they said they would buy for $X. They made me feel like I was being treated fairly."

"Oh no, Your Honor, I didn't get *anything* in writing. A confirmation? No, I didn't get one. A guarantee of payment? No, I didn't get that either. I just sent my coins and hoped for the best!"

Don't get further behind by trusting the same dealer who sold you down the river again. Don't confuse hope with reality. The problem is many dealers will tell you what you want to hear but won't perform. They want you to feel good and not question them.

Don't settle for this. It is easier to be lulled into believing everything is all right and not take action. It is hard to take the information I give you and act because you must face what you probably already suspect. Those you have continued to be placated have sat idly by while gold has gone up hundreds of percent.

As I write this there are Congressional hearings into major coin dealers. One Congressman has figured out that for investors buying overpriced semi-numismatic coins to make a profit, gold would have to continue going up the way it has for forty years!

Most people will know right away if their dealer is going to come through for them. You should really have a good idea within the first ten minutes of conversation. It's so simple to protect yourself.

Please remember, just because your dealer doesn't want to repurchase your coins doesn't mean he's a crook. It just means his business model is not set up to repurchase. Don't let an overeager salesperson turn it into a losing battle for you by promising what she can't deliver.

Don't count on future appreciation. You were already promised that. Every week, I hear from clients that their dealer told them to hold until the end of the year because the price will be up by then, or there is some reason that the price is increasing in the next two months.

These are stalling tactics. Please realize what they are before wasting your time.

Worse yet, savvy brokers use your wanting to sell to their advantage. They tell you they have a buyer, but he only wants complete sets. So, the dealer proceeds to try and sell you even more coins with the promise of selling your complete collection later.

Please don't believe it. It's a sham. You will simply be out more money. It's time to get a new dealer.

There are plenty of dealers like me out there who will gladly pay current market prices for your coins. Don't insist on going back to whom you bought the coins because they "should" buy them from you. If they give you any indication they are hesitant to buy your coins, go elsewhere. Trying to force the issue will cost you time and lots of money. It's time to get a new dealer.

Too many people get caught up in being "right" and think they can force the dealer to honor a buy back. It rarely is satisfying.

A dealer like me, who has a two-way market, will be happy to purchase your coins and work hard to please you.

Fly-by-Nights

I had a client in Quartzite, Arizona—a small old town near the border of Arizona and California. He had a sizeable amount of gold. It was basically gold bullion, but he thought it should be worth more than it was. Gold is gold is gold. We visited him, and he basically made a courtesy sell to us. He sold us about $35,000 of gold, since we took the trouble to go see him.

He told us he found somebody who would buy the rest of his gold, which was well in excess of a hundred thousand dollars, and pay more.

Three months later, his banker called my banker asking about a check that bounced, and he didn't know who was who and where to find them. The short version of the story is they called us because they still had our card and we had a number that worked. Our check cleared the bank immediately, so his banker was asking for our help. The seller had taken a check for over $100,000 from the other company (the company who said they'd pay more than we did—3 % more than us to be precise). Unfortunately, the check was written on a bank account that didn't exist. The company didn't exist. Be careful. Anybody can print a check and put a name on it. Check out the company before they show up at your door or before you mail your coins. You can do this by simply checking their association references, such as PNG, and ANA, or talking to their banker or local Better Business Bureau.

You Can Try to Do What We Do

The last option you have available to sell coins by yourself is try to duplicate what we do. Realize that good, quality dealers have many years of experience. My firm has over twenty years experience trading coins. You can go from dealer to dealer to dealer and schlep your coins all over town in the trunk of your car. Go from coin shop to coin shop to coin shop and find the best price.

You can do what we do, which is having a database of thousands of coin dealers, collectors, and investors. You can spend thousands of dollars a month on member dues for different organizations and attend all major coin shows.

You can find out who the best buyer for each coin is and whose check you can accept.

Travel to the dozens of different coin shows across the country to figure out which one is the best show to optimize your coin portfolio for the highest price.

When you sell your coins, you may have to take a loss, but you don't have to get pillaged and plundered. Your coins do have a value today, and there is a way to get cash for them in as little as twenty-four hours. But, you've got to know who to trust and to whom to turn.

Frankly, there are many good dealers out there. If you try, you can find them. It's a lot of work, but I beg you, don't give your coins away. Don't let someone take gross financial advantage of you. Do find an ethical coin dealer and get as much as your coins are truly worth.

The coin world is actually very small. The good dealers know who the other good dealers are.

It's a small world if you're an ethical insider. It's a cold, big, intimidating, foreboding, and dangerous world if you go at it naively, theoretically, or with more trust and innocence than you should. So, if you try to do what we do, be very careful and do your homework.

SECTION VII

IF YOU LOVE RARE COINS, GIVE YOURSELF A FIGHTING CHANCE

Maybe you just still want to be in rare coins. Here is how to save money and become an insider. You must become accountable for yourself and not deal with most brokers. To make it in rare coins, you have to be involved.

CHAPTER 29
THE SIX SIMPLE (REALLY SIMPLE) SECRETS OF COIN BUYING

Before You Buy

I can't tell you how often I hear people say, "I was taken advantage of," "He really cheated me," or, "That guy is a crook," only to hear later in the conversation, "I should've known better," "I should not have gotten into something I didn't understand," or, "I knew the minute I bought these coins it was a mistake."

What's my point?

I'm amazed that people spend $10,000, $20,000, $100,000, even $500,000 based on a phone call. It would be different if they did even a little bit of homework first.

It never ceases to amaze me to hear that people do so little research before they spend their money. Amazingly, they somehow know exactly what's going on after the check has been cashed. I can't tell you how many times I'll meet someone who paid $100,000 for $40,000 worth of coins. Then, when they want to sell, they become conscientious of every penny. Unfortunately, they can't make up the $60,000 loss by trying to recoup it on the sale. They already gave away more than what their entire real value is in commissions and markups. They believe that saving 5 % on the sale can make things better, but it can't. Even if they sold and paid no commission, it wouldn't help. The only thing that would have helped was if they had been diligent before the purchase. Buying right is perhaps the most important factor in coins.

Here's one unfortunate example.

I met an older woman at her home to look at some coins she had purchased only three months earlier. Actually, her son called, because he realized she had made a big mistake and wanted her out of coins. She had very little money and really needed to do some home improvements.

The coins she purchased for just under $30,000 were actually worth about $14,000. This was a mere three months later. The market had not really changed. The difference in price was simply the wholesale spread and retail markup!

During the ensuing phone conversations, all she could think of was trying to get me to cut my commission by 5 %. It's not that I object to negotiating—I don't. If she had done this up front when she purchased, she may have saved well over $10,000.

But now that the money was gone, I failed to see how an extra $700 was going to make her situation appreciably better. Don't get me wrong, every penny counts, but make it count before you give away your money.

No matter how good the broker's or dealer's story sounds, you need to remember to just say no. Then get off the phone, think about it, and if you still want to buy, it's time to do some homework.

Although I pick on dealers pretty hard in this book, the responsibility still lies with you, the buyer!

Despite everything I've told you and will tell you in the remainder of this book, coins can be fun and even profitable if you do it right. Like any other investment, timing is critical and price is everything.

If you pay the right price going in, you're ten steps ahead of the average investor.

Most people wouldn't buy a house without checking out the market first and comparing prices. Most probably wouldn't even buy a car without doing some research and knowing what they wanted to pay. Everyone would probably negotiate a price on either of these and not just pay the asking price. Most people even do this for something simple, like a washing machine or refrigerator.

Yet, a coin dealer calls and gives a song-and-dance or an emotional appeal and says you need to buy right now, and smart, normally cautious people buy on the spot.

Let me give you the six critical secrets to buying coins. Please remember there are always exceptions to anything in rare coins, but these secrets should help keep you safe.

SECRET #1: Don't be pressured. Hang up and think about the purchase. If it still makes sense, call a few dealers and ask them, "What's Grey Sheet on this coin?" And, of course, only buy coins certified by PCGS or NGC.

You'll be surprised how easy it is to find a wholesale price. Dealers will immediately believe you know something about coins when you mention the Grey Sheet! The Grey Sheet is actually the Coin Dealer Newsletter and is used by every dealer in the country. If it's what they use, it should be what you use.

Keep in mind the Grey Sheet uses auctions, teletype trades, bids, show sales, and other reported sales to come up with an average price. So, not every price is 100 % accurate, but they are the best in the industry. The people who publish it take a lot of time and painstaking effort to make sure they are offering the best information available.

As I've already mentioned, every dealer in the country uses the *Coin Dealer Newsletter* and you should, too. It's easy to find, so there's no excuse not to.

Now that you know the wholesale price of a coin, it should be easy to decide if you're being offered a good deal. If you're within 10 % or 15 %, maybe even 20% of the Grey Sheet, it's probably priced right. This does not mean it is a good coin to buy, only that it is priced right.

This simple step could've saved investors that I've met over the past twenty years at least $400,000,000.

If you buy right, you've won 70 % of the battle. That's how easy it is. Two or three calls and fewer than twenty minutes of your time is all it would take. It really doesn't matter who you call for the information, as long as you ask about the Grey Sheet. You can call PNG for dealers' names and phone numbers or simply look under "Coin Dealers" in your Yellow Pages. For reference purposes, I've included PNG's address and phone number in the Glossary.

SECRET #2: Ask for a discount!

When you buy a car or house, you negotiate the price. Why wouldn't you ask for a break on a coin?

I don't mean you should try to negotiate on $25 or $100 coins—you wouldn't get anywhere. But, if you spend a couple thousand dollars and certainly tens of thousands of dollars, all you need to do is ask. I learned this simple rule when I was twelve years old. Instead of paying the asking price in a magazine for a coin I needed to complete a collection, I called the dealer and got a discount.

Real dealers go to shows and also negotiate with other dealers by phone or in person. They're used to it. It's the way the business runs.

Of course, if you're just dealing with a broker or salesperson, she may have little knowledge or control of the price. But even then, tell her you want a better price. Typically, a broker or salesperson will ask the boss and provide an answer for you.

I believe that by simply asking, you can expect to save 5 % to 10 % off the quoted price!

CAUTION: Only do this after you have checked prices as in Secret #1 and you've decided you really want to buy the coin(s). Do not take this step first, because you may still overpay.

Example: Dealer F quotes you $1,000 for a coin with a Grey Sheet value of $700. You get a 5 % discount, and your cost is $950. You still paid a whopping 36 % over wholesale. This is a terrible investment, no matter how good the coin is!

By knowing the wholesale price is $700, you don't want to pay more than $800 to $840. Then ask for a discount. Now, you'll only need the coin to go up 10 % to 15% before you start making money.

SECRET #3: Never buy based on so-called catalog prices or retail prices without doing more research.

Please realize that the coins sold on TV are usually priced very, very high if you're buying them for investment purposes. The TV shopping networks do provide a valuable service for collectors, but their expenses are likely to be very high, so their prices must reflect this. As an investor, you simply can't afford the premium. As a collector, it may well be worth the price to shop from home and have the convenience of buying this way. Plus, it's a lot of fun.

You can't afford to pay retail for an investment. Most retail prices are 35 % to 100% or more over bid prices. If you are a collector and just absolutely need a specific coin, you may have to pay these prices, but that is the only exception.

However, as an investor, it's very, very rare that you absolutely have to buy any specific coin. There are more "rare coins" out there than you could imagine.

Be weary of dealers offering you coins at catalog or Internet pricing. These prices are generally showing you high retail and are reflections of prices at which dealers advertise their coins.

Remember, any coin newspaper or magazine depends on advertising for its revenue. When they list coin values, they must list values high enough so that their advertisers don't look as if they are overpricing coins. Likewise, most of the Internet sites I've seen to date tend to list prices, which allow for heavy markups.

This does not mean that these institutions are crooked or misleading. It's simply a fact of which you need to be aware. They are truly providing a valuable service. It's up to you to decide if they are providing prices you want to pay.

In the 1980s, a large dealer published his own price list. It was not an accurate sample of what prices were market wide. He published his price list on a regular basis and gave the impression that the coins he sold were going up 15 to 20 % a year. The problem was, his prices were eventually so unrealistic compared with the actual market, that when people tried to sell them back to him, they could not get his fictitious price. He was forced out of business, and the investors were left holding the bag.

The best way to follow your values and make sure you're receiving a fair price is to get a copy of the *Coin Dealer Newsletter*, especially before you purchase, because once you overpay, you can never get back that money.

SECRET #4: Only buy coins listed in the weekly or monthly Grey Sheets.

Although there are always exceptions, only buying coins listed in the weekly or monthly Grey Sheets is a good general rule to follow, unless you become very specialized in an area that interests you, such as Charlotte or Dahlonega Mint coins. The reason will become obvious when you go to sell.

The Grey Sheet is available as a weekly, monthly, and quarterly publication. Different coins are reported in each one. Simple logic tells you that the coins reported in a weekly time frame are the most actively traded coins. It follows that they are also the most liquid and widely recognized. The quarterly reports on the least-traded coins. Which coins would you rather own?

By sticking to the most actively traded and most in demand, you increase your chances of making money. You can see that, thus far, with only four simple secrets, we have substantially narrowed the field of what you should buy and what you should pay. It's easy so far, and you are already heads and tails above 90 % of the average investors!

SECRET #5: Ask about recent performance.

Ask your dealer what's happened to certain coins or coin areas over the past year or two. If the coins you are looking at have gone up 50 %, it may be a red flag, unless we are in a red-hot coin market, which we haven't been since 1989.

If a coin has gone up 50 to 100 % or more, it will be very tempting for dealers and investors to sell into this move. But at best, prices could stall, and at worst, they could, and usually do, tumble.

A pertinent follow-up question to any dealer would be, "Has anyone been promoting these coins?" If the answer is yes, it's another red flag, unless the promoter has just begun his promotion.

Instead, find out if any series or types of coins have been moving up a few percentage points a month. I love these coins, because prices can move up for a year or two at 2 to 4 % a month, and no one ever notices because it's so gradual. Better still, you don't normally get the selling pressure.

All of this information is available through *Coin Dealer Newsletter* or knowledgeable dealers. However, don't expect a broker or salesperson to know all of it, though he may know which coin is "hot" or has gone up 50 % or 100 %, because chances are, that's exactly what he's selling.

In my experience, you want to sell, not buy, when coins go up 50 to 100 %.

Buy at the beginning of a big move, which is often indicated by many small moves.

SECRET #6: Sell.

You will never know exactly when to sell, whether it's coins, stocks, gold, real estate, or antique cars. You need a dealer who will monitor your coins and let you know when they go up and be willing to sell them for you. You will be amazed at how many dealers promise this but never deliver. It's true! Many dealers detest the idea of buying back your coins. In fact, many outright. You will never know exactly when to sell, whether it's coins, stocks, gold, real estate, or antique cars. You need a dealer who will monitor your coins and let you know when they go up and be willing to sell them for you. You will be amazed at how many dealers promise this but never deliver. It's true! Many dealers detest the idea of buying back your coins. In fact, many outright refuse to do so.

You need to take some responsibility for forcing the issue, and I've given you ways that you can.

Another tact you should take is when an area of the market is touted as being "hot," sell into it.

You can also ask your dealer to provide annual or semiannual updates for you. Tell them you want the Bid prices so you know where you stand.

Please realize that most dealers will provide this on request. This means that you need to be prepared to call every six months or year to request it.

Before you purchase, make it clear to your dealer that you expect this service and send your request in writing. If possible, have the dealer put it in writing, too, so there are no misunderstandings or hurt feelings later.

These simple steps will not guarantee you a profit. While they are certainly simplified for reasons of this book, they will save you thousands of dollars.

CHAPTER 30
HOW TO MAKE MONEY

Five Rules You Must Follow

Successful coin investing is simple. All you have to do to turn the odds in your favor is religiously follow a handful of rules.

Rule #1: Master Supply and Demand

First, determine what is driving the demand. Then determine the supply of available coins. This is where 99 % of all investors go wrong. They buy what the dealer says is rare and in demand and take his word for it.

Most dealers sell you what they can buy in large quantities and hide a high profit margin. Those are the last coins you want to buy. Two examples are Patterns and California gold. Read publications like *Coin World*, the *Coin Dealer Newsletter*, and the *Numismatic News*. Attend auctions and coin shows and talk to several respected dealers. Stay away from the mountain of self-serving newsletters and junk mail touting "great buys."

Rule #2: Invest Time Before Money

To make money, you must first decide which coins to buy. The best way of doing this is to follow collector trends. You must do at least a minimal amount of research to determine fair prices. It's simple; I'll give you a recent example.

A dealer was quoting certain gold coins at $3,500 each in MS-65 quality. I won't reveal the coin, because my intention is not to pick on any particular dealer(s). At the time, he gave a lot of reasons why the coin should increase in value. The reasons were actually good ones, and he was correct in his outlook.

However, when a client called around, he was able to

purchase that coin for $1,900 (about $300 over wholesale). I recommended he purchase at $1,900, and he did. Within the year, the bid on the coin went up substantially, and he was able to sell that coin for $2,700.

The point is this: the reasons the dealer gave him to buy were right on the money. The problem was that the dealer was too high on the price, by 85 %. If this buyer had not done his research, he would have lost $800 (23 %) within a year, even though the market value of the coin went up $1,100!

Instead, by making a few calls, he was able to buy at the right price and eventually pocket $800—a tidy 42 % profit.

Rule #3: Learn When to Hold Them and When to Fold Them

With each of your investments, decide on a time frame and/or price where you'd like to get out. And decide under what condition you'll consider taking a loss and moving on.

Patience is a necessity, but I've seen literally thousands of investors hold losing coins for ten, fifteen, or twenty-five years in hopes of someday breaking even. The same dealers who sold them the loser coins in the first place often urged them to continue holding them, claiming profits were, "right around the corner."

Keep in mind that coins are not the most liquid asset. In fact, PCGS, one of the premier coin-grading services, adds this disclaimer in all advertisements:

> *Certification by PCGS does not guarantee protection against the normal risks associated with potentially volatile markets. The degree of liquidity of PCGS certified coins will vary according to general market conditions and according to the particular coin involved. For some coins there may be no active market at all at certain points in time.*

If you suddenly need cash for medical or other reasons, or you have any other unforeseen and immediate need to sell your coins, this might not be the best investment for you.

Rule #4: Learn from Collectors

Before I became a professional dealer, I was a collector. When I started collecting in the late 1960s, I learned how to buy and sell within the context of collectibles. First, determine which coins the collectors as a group have a history of collecting, whether by series or type of coin. Then, buy the rarer coins in these collectible groups in high grade and pull them off the market. As the collectors slowly bid up the prices over a few years, sell back into the market via a dealer or coin show. Very simple.

Rule #5: Learn from Dealers

Besides collectors, the only other group that regularly makes money is dealers, but they don't hold: they buy and sell. Never forget that.

CHAPTER 31
THE THREE R's OF COIN INVESTING

It's very confusing to novice investors to figure out which coins have real collector/investment potential. It seems as if it becomes even more confusing listening to brokers. They often use one criterion to convince an investor that a coin should be purchased while ignoring others.

Often, an investor will hear that a coin has low mintage, a small population (the number of coins graded by PCGS and/or NGC),
and relatively cheap price compared to other coins with the same rarity, condition, pedigrees, and so on.

The real answer to what constitutes an investment coin is a combination of factors. No one factor alone determines whether a coin is a good buy or potential investment.

A coin can be very rare, but if no one wants to collect it, the price will not rise. A coin can be very popular but be available in such high quantities that the price does not rise.

There are three simple criteria I use to evaluate any coin I intend to buy.

Rarity

This is perhaps the most obvious factor. It is also the most misused. Many unsuspecting investors have been talked into purchasing extremely "rare" coins yet have lost huge amounts of money.

Obviously, coins with mintages in the millions or populations in the thousands cannot be considered rare. The tricky thing about population is that it constantly changes.

When hoards are discovered, populations soar. Also, when prices go up, people tend to get more coins certified in order to sell. Higher prices always bring more coins onto the market. Thus, populations rise.

There are countless examples of populations increasing hundreds, if not thousands of percent, when prices doubled or more in the late 1980s and early 1990s.

So, even rarity can't be taken for granted; anytime there is a substantial rise in price, the population rarity must be checked. Low-mintage coins are a good place to start evaluating rarity. For example, when looking at mintages of Morgan Silver Dollars, one will see many dates with mintages of one million or more! However, scanning the mintage figures, you will notice the 1895 coin has a mintage of 880 pieces. This is definitely rare. There is also an abundance of ways to compare relative rarity within a series. One method I used when I was only ten years old was very good.

Multiply the price with the mintage; the smaller the number, the greater the relative rarity. This method actually provided me with a lot of winners! The easiest way to find mintages is the Red Book—A Guide Book of United States Coins.

But this method must be combined with the next two criteria. Also, it is important to note that super-rarity can often work against you. Sometimes a coin is so rare, so elusive, that collectors or dealers don't think they will ever have a chance to find one. Therefore, no one ever bids up the price for you. This happens frequently on coins that are super high grade or coins that have populations fewer than ten coins. So, it's something of which to be aware.

Recognizable Coins

Many coins are rare but not readily recognized by the average collector/investor or even dealer.

There are an abundance of rare date coins ranging from 1 cent to $20 gold pieces minted in the 1800s. Unfortunately, very few collectors put these sets together. This means that even if you have the only one of a certain rarity, if no one is collecting it, the coin will not appreciate.

I've seen people who have purchased extremely rare coins from not only the United States but all over the world. For example, one collector purchased African coins that had mintages of less than twenty coins. The catalog values were fairly high, but when he wanted to sell, he couldn't find a buyer. He commented to me that the only thing rarer than his coins was somebody to buy them! You want coins that a large number of collectors and dealers recognize and collect.

You don't want a coin that you have to explain to a collector. For example, any dealer or collector will recognize 1909-SVDB or 1914-D or 1955/55 as truly rare Lincoln Cents. However, few will recognize an 1864 Seated Liberty Dime as a rare coin, even though it actually is many times rarer than the
coins previously mentioned.

Collector trends determine which coins are recognizable. Stay away from short- term or emerging trends such as modern coins in MS-69 or MS-70. It's much too early to tell if this is just another fad. Plus, many modern coins are readily available in these high grades because of improved minting processes. Established collector trends and rarity will provide the least amount of risk, while also providing the best chance at appreciation.

Resale Market

This really goes hand in hand with the first two factors. The reason is, if you pick the right coins, combining collector recognition with rarity, the result should be a ready resale market. Please look at this closely. If you believe you have found a good candidate coin to buy, make sure the resale market is healthy. You could call dealers or look at a weekly Grey Sheet to help determine this.

If you find that dealers don't clamor to give you a bid on the coin, you probably have chosen the wrong coin.

CHAPTER 32
HOW TO USE DEALER PROMOS TO PROFIT

The coin market has changed substantially over the past twenty-five years. I've noticed that with fewer and fewer serious investors and collectors in the market, the potential for profits has also narrowed. Many argue that the number of collectors and investors is actually growing. But a simple look at what has happened to both buyers and sellers tells a far different story.

Many of the investors from the early 1980s are now seventy, eighty, and even ninety years of age. For the most part, they are not today's buyers. While there is certainly some interest in coins from my generation, they are not nearly as popular as with the previous one.

Simply look at some of the large dealers who used to employ hundreds of brokers. They are lucky if they have twenty or thirty in today's market. I submit that this is due to the declining number of investors.

While we all have heard about collector demand or investor panic driving the market, dealers say little about the legal manipulation.

In fact, many dealers don't even understand they are manipulating prices. Many times, if a dealer is large enough or has a sufficient marketing program, they can influence the market they promote. By creating the demand, dealers essentially fulfill their own predictions.

Understanding how this happens can mean the difference between being one of the many who buy at the highs and never break even, or buying early and making a profit.

This is truly speculating as opposed to actual investing or hedging. But there is more money to be made with much less risk if you can manage to do it correctly.

Conversely, if you already own coins, you may be able to recoup more of your money if you are lucky enough to own coinsthat become promoted.

ALWAYS SELL INTO STRENGTH

I've been derided for telling people to "sell into strength." The fact is in the vast majority of market moves, an investor would come out way ahead by selling when everyone else is clamoring to buy. This is not just true in coins and bullion but also in stocks, bonds, and real estate. Just look at the "tech bubble" and crash of the 1990s and 2000.

What keeps people from selling is the fear that the market may suddenly take off, and they may miss out on a once-in-a-lifetime run-up. Unfortunately, that's about how often the major run-ups happen—once in a lifetime. I find it much more prudent to sell when a market goes up than to bet on a one in a thousand chance of a runaway market.

It is true that we have had a handful of these runaways, but few people have profited. Greed sets in, and most people hold through the gain and watch it tumble right back down. Then they wait for history to repeat itself, always hoping they'll get just one more chance.

That's why people are always waiting for higher prices. Then, when they get them, they wait again. When investors miss their chance to sell at a top, they often time freeze or panic and do nothing.

WHAT IS A DEALER PROMO?

A dealer promo is basically what it says. A dealer or group of dealers will choose a coin or type of coin they believe is rare, desirable, available, and promote it. Sometimes it will be a fairly common item, like silver dollars. Other times, it will be rarer or even a modern item. The key is it must be something not currently "in favor" in the market. After all, no dealer would promote a coin they aren't able to buy enough of to resell. The idea is simple, but you must observe some strict rules.

Buy coins when a large promotion starts—not after you've heard about it for a year.

Sometimes a tip-off will be a marketer's new book about a certain area of the market. Or, it could be a media blitz in a variety of newsletters or even a flood of phone calls urging the promoted coins.

The key is to get in early, before sales take off—if they do. If the promotion is successful, you may see almost immediate appreciation.

Be wary of buying the coins from the dealers actually doing the promotion without checking with a few other dealers for prices.

Many times, markups are 50 to 100 % over wholesale, and you'll never make money that way. Before you buy, call a few dealers for competitive prices. Check the *Coin Dealer Newsletter* prices (refer to how to buy right in chapter 30). Once you've decided to take the plunge and have checked pricing, buy only the coins you have predetermined; don't be talked into something else.

Keep in mind, this is speculative. It won't work every time.

Sometimes promos fail, and the dealer sales don't push up the market. If the market doesn't start moving, it's better to sell and move on before the dealer gives up and starts dumping coins.

If your coins do rise, don't be afraid to take a profit,

especially once prices stagnate. Otherwise, you may get stuck holding the bag as dealers move on to new promos.

A final caution. You must be responsible for watching prices if you deal with a broker.

It is rare that a dealer running a promo will ever tell you to sell. They can't. If they told clients to sell, they would collapse the market they just built up.

While there certainly is no sure thing when it comes to making money in coins, this strategy can often provide decent returns for a small risk. Remember, if you do this right, you are buying coins that are out of favor; therefore prices should be near the lows. If the promo fails, you haven't paid the big premiums for an overheated market, so your loss should be limited to the spread you paid. Hopefully, if you do your homework, that spread will be 10 to 20 %.

If the promo works, you may make a nice profit. One dealer promo we took advantage of was a coin that went from $1,700 to $6,100 in fewer than five years. As I write this book, the price has stabilized, as I believe the promo has run its course.

Another example concerned the U.S. Gold in MS-65. A well-known newsletter writer had touted these coins as being worthwhile investments. Certain large dealers quickly followed his recommendation by heavily promoting these coins. In just three weeks, many coins rose about 20 %.

Try this strategy only if you are willing to be serious about getting a decent price when you buy and spending the time to monitor prices afterward.

CHAPTER 33
BEST BETS TO MAKE MONEY

Collectors are ultimately taking back the coin market, but rare coins have continued to do well in many cases. An extreme example is the classic 1913 Liberty Nickel. In 1967, this coin sold for $13,000, which was a fortune at the time. In 1998, it sold for $1,400,000 and then $1,840,000 in 2000. In 2003, a wonderfully orchestrated campaign to find the last missing coin (there were only five made and only four accounted for) actually brought a wave of new interest as the last coin was actually found. A well-known and well-respected dealer purchased a 1913 Liberty Nickel for $3,000,000. Crazy as it may sound, even though his coin is far from the finest of the five known, he could likely turn a quick $500,000 to $1 million profit.

Of course, most people don't have millions to invest, but the point is this coin is considered one of the kings of U.S. coins. Every dealer and collector is aware of it. When the five coins were put on display, thousands clamored for the chance just to see them. Since the 1990s, million dollar coins appear and trade on a more frequent basis.

The safest and easiest way to "invest" in rare coins is to become a collector. That means to educate yourself about which coins are truly rare, recognized collectibles and to buy the best while avoiding esoteric material.

There are many areas of the market that hold promise. And, if you actually enjoy rare coins, great coins can be found in any area.

What to buy is a function of how much a person can comfortably spend. Do not scrape together your last dime to buy coins, and please, do not purchase with a credit card and hope the coin(s) will appreciate fast enough to make money and pay off the card.

If you have $10 million to spend, by all means buy a few of the ultra-rare multimillion dollar coins, for example, the 1913 Liberty

Nickel, 1804 Bust $1; they are the most likely to be sure bets. The coin market appears to be reverting to true collectors. It will begin to resemble the art market, fewer buyers, but these buyers will be more focused and more serious.

Even though you constantly hear of paintings selling in the tens of millions, you are rarely told that everyone should buy rare art. Why is it that everyone should buy rare coins? The true collector coins will continue to hold their own and likely appreciate.

Most people want specific examples of coins to buy. Contrary to parts of this book, there are hundreds of coins from which to choose. It's just that many of the brokers calling you on the phone will seldom sell them to you at a reasonable price. Usually, they are trying to sell their best guess at investment coins.

This is speculating not investing. Recently, at least a handful of large, high-profile dealers have started to concentrate on truly rare collectible coins. I think this is a very positive sign for this market.

I believe this is only possible because there are fewer buyers than there were twenty years ago. In the past, it was impossible to have one hundred to two hundred brokers selling rare coins. They had to sell what is considered semi-rare or common coins. But now, it is rare to find more than thirty brokers at any one dealer. This new structure readily avails itself to selling true rarities.

If you decide to buy, do your homework first.

Get at least a rudimentary education; buy a *Red Book* and glance at different series of coins. Please refer to Section VII for more details.

1. Morgan silver dollars are one of the most collected areas of the coin market.

While I do not recommend anything common or even semi-rare, many coins in this category do qualify as "investments." Surely, the most rare and sought after is the 1895-P Morgan, of which only 880 were made. Even in the extremely low grade of VG (see Glossary for explanation of grades), this coin has skyrocketed from $6,000 to $15,000 in only a few years. Other rare dates include, but are not limited to, 1879-CC, 1889-CC, 1884-S, 1892-S, 1893-S, 1895-O, 1901-P, 1903-S, and 1904-S. A quick glance through the Red Book or Coin Dealer Newsletter will make it obvious as to which coins are rare. To a great degree, simply looking at the price will reveal this.

However, please take note that some of these only become rare and potentially profitable in MS-60 or higher quality, unlike the low-grade potential of the 1895-P or even 1893-S. Most series include some rare dates. I would look to the most collected series to start:

- Lincoln Cents
- Buffalo Nickels
- Mercury Dimes
- Walking Liberty Halves
- Morgan Dollars
- $5 Indian Head Gold
- $10 Indian Gold

This list is meant to only be a starting point, as there are many coins and types of coins that are collectable and desirable, going all the way back to 1792. These earlier coins do require a bit more research, though.

2. Rare dates in highly collected series—such as 1916-D, 1921, and 1921-D Mercury Dimes.

- Rare date Lincoln Cent such as 1909-SVDB, 1914-D, and 1955/55; rare date Buffalo Nickels such as 1938-D Three-Legged, 1916/16, 1918-17D, to name a few.
- Early rare date Walking Liberty Halves, including but not limited to, 1921-P, 1921-D, 1921-S, and many earlier dates,

again in higher quality—MS-63 or better.

- Standing Liberty Quarters such as 1916, 1918/17-S, and 1927-S.
- Even some of the more modern Washington Quarters such as 1932-D, 1932-S, 1934-D, and 1934-S, will likely turn out to be good performers.

This is by no means a complete list. It is merely a starting place. Any collector would surely recognize any coin mentioned, which is the point.

Quantity vs. Quality

In most cases, I would prefer to have fewer but rarer coins. The coins noted in the previous section range from $2,000 to almost $200,000 each.

Don't be afraid of having more expensive coins as long as they are well recognized. They are likely to be the rarest and hardest to find. Therefore, the upward pressure can be greater. I'm always amazed when someone tells me they bought "rare" coins and then proceed to show me twenty, thirty, even one hundred of the same coin.

If dealers can sell rolls or large groups of coins, how rare can they possibly be?

Also, keep in mind if you have one hundred common coins, they will move in price together. In other words, they would move as one. Either they all go up, they all go down, or they all do nothing. Don't fool yourself into believing that having many coins diversifies your portfolio or lessens your risk. You'd be better off with a handful of rare coins.

CHAPTER 34
SELLING FOR A PROFIT

I still believe people can make money in coins. The biggest problem is they're trying to do it by talking to promoters and paying double what the coins are worth. They are relying solely on the sellers of the coins and are not spending time ensuring that the information is correct. In other words, they are not doing their homework.

I think for the right people, not the majority of people, coins still make sense.

Collectors

Who does make money and how? In my experience, more than ninety-five out of a hundred people—most of whom have not done the work required—have lost and will continue to lose on their coin investments on a perennial basis.

However, five percent or less do not. But those five percent are a special breed, and maybe you're one of them. Let's talk about who they are, what they do, how they think, and what and how they buy. I've consistently seen certain characteristics in this five percent.

There are a couple of different categories of people who make money in coins. The people who tend to make the most money in rare coins tend to be true collectors or dealers. Dealers make money for one good reason: they don't hold, they buy and sell.

The collector is the person who might subconsciously say, "I'm going to buy something that's going to go up in value." But he is also the person who says, "I love U.S. Silver Dollars," or, "I love Commemorative coins." He loves the history. He loves the coins. The reason that most of us dealers got into this business was because we were collectors when we were kids.

I know I never got into collecting to try and make money, although it was certainly exciting when it happened. Collectors love the history. They love the look, the feel of coins, and they really come alive when they relate to the coin. I remember the first coins I found that really got me excited. I found some Lincoln cents from 1909 and 1914. I thought, *"Wow! Just think about whose hands they went through and what was going on when they were made, Teddy Roosevelt was president."* One of my dad's friends was a coin collector and he gave me a one-cent piece from 1797. He told me, "This coin was around when we were a brand new nation ... just think who could have held this coin."

The history was just so intriguing. It's the same reason people collect cars, antiques, and art. They collect them not so much to make money. They collect them because they love the object, just like any other collectible.

The majority of those who make money are the true collectors, because the collectors are buying what they love. You can get lucky. If you're in the right place at the right time, you can make money. But that's the once-in-a-lifetime chance, like the coin market or the gold and silver market in 1979/1980. The market was so hot it didn't matter what you had; you had a chance to make money, depending on whom you bought from and what you paid, of course.

Everything went up. The fact is those types of markets don't come around very often. So, to buy coins and expect the market to boom and bail you out, practically guarantees your loss. A collector is going to buy what he likes. That's the reason the coin market initially started to appreciate. Investors looked at the coin market because they could see prices going up year after year on certain highly collected coins.

The collectors ran up the price on themselves, because a majority of collectors wanted the same coins if there was something historically significant, or if it was something they needed to fill a set. A majority of collectors needed the coin, so they ran up the price.

An example: A collector, putting together a set of Lincoln cents, will most likely have the most common coins because they are easy to get. Consequently, most people acquire them first. They end up with those five holes in the collection that every other collector also needs. So, at some point, you have to buy those five coins to fill your set. From the time I was twelve years old, I'd watch the coins I needed to find to fill those five slots. The 1909 SVDB is the rarest one, and I'd watch it and I'd watch it. It would go up $10. And then the next time, "Oh, it went up another $10." Finally, I'd say, "I better buy it before it goes up again."

When I was twelve years old, I bought my first 1909 SVDB Penny for $70. Today, the same coin costs $500 to $600. I didn't get rich holding it for thirty plus years, but that's the idea—the collectors are going to buy it. So, if you're a collector, you're going to gravitate to those coins not because it's thought out, but because you are collecting what you like.

The Difference Between Collecting and Investing

The collector is the market. An investor is trying to beat the market.

Collectors tend to focus on different coins than investors. And when the collectors see the price has dropped, they buy, because they're not saying, "The bottom's dropping out." They're looking at it and saying, "Wow, now I can afford ten coins instead of three coins."

Collectors are patient; they wait for what they want. Frequently, dealers will make a lot of money selling coins to collectors, because they'll pay whatever it takes if it's a coin they want. It has to be rare. There can't be a million of them out there, otherwise, the buyer has the leverage.

True collectors are extremely well educated regarding coins.

If I meet a collector who specializes in one small area in the market, they'll often know more than I do. I'll get a collector who says, "All I collect are Bust half-dollars." That's all he does in his spare time. I guarantee you this guy is going to know every variety and every nuance about these Bust halves. And somebody who's really committed to being a collector is somebody who's willing to commit the time. It's not an inexpensive hobby. But, if somebody's willing to do the research and learn about coins, yes, they can make money.

Investors

The problem with most investors is they don't want to take the time to learn about the coin market, not even the basics. They just want to hand their money to somebody and have it done. I did that in the stock market, as I mentioned in an earlier chapter, and I can tell you from my experience, it doesn't work any better in stocks than it does in coins.

If an investor wanted to take the time, there's an abundance of information that's easy to find. It's not the same as it was in the 1970s and 1980s. Now you can find out how many of each coin were graded by PCGS or NGC simply by purchasing a Population Report from them. You can tell how many there were five years ago, how many there are now. You could chart prices, and with a little research, see who or what caused many of the increases and declines in prices.

For the right people with the right strategy and long-term commitment, it can be a rewarding experience and financially profitable.

The point I want to make here is most people I come across did not invest with that in mind. Their motives were honorable, but they bought out of fear and often on the spur of the moment, taking only the broker's word for it over the phone. Their purchases were well intended, but their results were very disappointing. For people with that mind-set, I can't urge them or convince them fast enough to get out of the market and stay out.

I could tell you how to save a substantial amount of money. If someone was going to spend $100,000, I could show them how to buy those coins and save as little as $20,000 and as much as $40,000 in the majority of cases. And that's with only a week's worth of effort.

When you buy at the right price to start with, 70 % of the problems are taken care of. Most of the investors I see bought from somebody who hyped them on the phone. They bought because the broker scared them or promised them something—some unbelievable profit or protection for some perceived calamity. That's the main problem investors have. I can't urge you enough to do your homework and find a good, honest dealer. They are out there. And they are typically not calling you every month with a "hot buy."

SECTION VIII

QUESTIONS FROM CLIENTS

CHAPTER 35
FREQUENTLY ASKED QUESTIONS

I've compiled the most frequently asked questions I get on the phone, on the road, or when I sit down and look at people's portfolios. I get asked these questions from people who are either invested in coins, want to figure out what to do with the coins they have now, or are thinking about investing in the first place. I've given the best-reasoned, best-informed answers I can.

Q. My dealer insists you're wrong about buying better date or rare date $20 gold Liberties or other esoteric coins because they have low population numbers. Why?

A. Low population numbers. What that means: PCGS and NGC keep track of how many of each coin are graded. This is the population. PCGS and NGC publish these numbers every month. A lot of dealers will sell a coin and say, "Look at this coin. There are only ten graded. There are only twenty graded," or, "This is the only one graded." And that quantity is called the population.

That number may grow in the future as they find more coins, or it may not. We don't know that. It shows you only one factor you need to consider when investing in the coin: it's showing you a perceived rarity. The problem you have when you look at population numbers alone is they don't tell you if there's actually a demand for the coin. You could have the only coin graded, but if no collector wants it, it doesn't really matter; there's no demand for it.

Let me give you an example. Let's look at a Seated Liberty quarter, minted between 1851 and 1891. There are very, very few people who collect that by series. This means they don't collect every date and every mint mark of the series. Same thing goes with the $20 Liberties and $10 Liberties and most Type coins prior to 1916. Very few people will collect the whole set and have a complete set of $20 Liberties, or these other coins, that include every year and every mintmark. The reasons are (1) it's almost impossible, and (2) it's so financially restrictive that very few people could afford to buy every coin in the series. So what's evolved is the collectors tend to go toward the series they can actually buy and assemble. Typically, they include more modern sets like Buffalo nickels, Lincoln cents, Walking Liberty half-dollars, 50 pence. Silver Commemoratives, Gold Commemoratives, Peace Dollars, Morgan Dollars, Mercury Dimes, or type sets, which are simply one of each kind of coin.

In the example of the Seated Liberty quarters, an 1875 is worth the same as an 1890 or an 1891 or an 1887. It doesn't matter, because almost no one collects them by date. In other words, they're collected by type. Someone will say, "I want a Type II $20 Liberty," or, "I want a Barber quarter." What they're saying is they want any date. They'll take any date, but they want that type of coin. And that's the way the collectors buy. They'll buy one of each kind of coin as opposed to one of every date and mintmark of the coin.

When you look at the population, it may make a coin look very, very rare, but what you need to do is look at the population for the entire series. So, you might be looking at how many coins are graded in a certain quality for forty years of minting. And instead of fourteen, that number might all of a sudden jump to five thousand.

The population tells you nothing more than how many coins of that particular coin are graded. It tells you the coin is rare, but that doesn't tell you if there's any demand for the coin, if it's a recognized coin, if there's a market for the coin, or if anyone's bidding on the coin. You need to know all of that information, or your dealer needs to know. The population is certainly important when you look at a coin. If a coin has a population of a hundred thousand, it is automatically something you don't want to look at. If a coin has a population of a hundred, fifty, ten to two hundred, all that tells me as an investor is, "Now I want to look at something further. It passed one criteria. Let's see how the other five criteria add up."

Q. What about taking prices off the Internet sites?

A. At this time, I do not know of an Internet site that lists the wholesale prices or bid prices that are readily available without a subscription. If anyone knows of such a site, they're welcome to call me and tell me about it. The reason I keep talking about wholesale or bid prices is the only price that's important to an investor is the price they could sell it for, not the price they could buy it for.

PCGS has an Internet pricing section. I believe the prices are very inflated compared to the price you could actually sell the coins. The prices are high retail and, in my opinion, allow for high markups. In many cases, you could probably buy the coins for 30 to 40 % less. One of my clients uses the PCGS prices to bid on e-Bay. He bids 20 % less than the PCGS site and said he almost always gets the coin. I believe that confirms the prices are too high. Even at 20 % less, he is probably paying too much.

The Internet sites I've seen price coins as much as 40 to 300 % more than the coin is worth if you had to turn around and resell it. As of this writing, I have not found anything on the Internet that gives you actual liquidation prices; only high retail can be found.

Q. How do I get reliable prices?

A. There are actually two ways the average guy on the street can get a very good idea of true value. There's the certified quote system, which is the system the dealers actually list their bids on—bids and asks. In other words, we offer coins for sale and we offer to buy coins sight-unseen and sight-seen on this system. The problem for the average investor is it's very expensive. It's going to cost in the neighborhood of $300 to $500 a month. For most people, that's not going to work. If you have a good relationship with your dealer, you might be able to call and ask them to look up prices on a particular coin. I don't do it every single day, but you could call and say, "Nick, what's this coin going for right now?" And I can look it up on the quote system and tell you exactly what the bid is at that minute.

If you're going to invest over $5,000, you should invest $117 and subscribe to the Certified *Coin Dealer Newsletter*, otherwise known as the "Blue Sheet" or the *Coin Dealer Newsletter*, known as the "Grey Sheet". It's cheap, and it's very good, because the owners spend a lot of time researching prices. It may not tell you exactly to the penny what that coin is worth, but here's a good example of how to use it. A client of ours paid $6,000 for an 1874 Carson City minted $20 gold piece from another dealer without first checking prices. The coin was graded AU58, which means "About Uncirculated." It's not quite a new coin; it's a high-grade circulated coin. I pulled out the *Coin Dealer Newsletter*. This is what every single dealer in the country uses when valuing coins.

We looked up the price for this coin. Listed under MS-60, which is a full grade higher than the coin this client was sold, was a price of $5,500. The price for an AU coin was $1,400. Knowing that the next grade higher than his coin was listed for $500 less than he was charged, convinced him the price he was charged was way out of line.

The third way you can find out prices on coins is to call the Professional Numismatic Guild (PNG) in Fallbrook, California. Their phone number is (760) 728-1300, and you can get two to five dealers' names. You can call them and ask them what price they would buy or sell a specific coin. Even if they don't have it, they would have access to the two systems I just told you about, and they can give you a good idea. The reason I'm recommending PNG is, in my opinion, that's the best group of dealers out there. They're screened, they sign agreements, and they're professionals. Those are three easy ways to get accurate prices. The most time consuming of them takes fifteen minutes of your time, yet it can save you thousands or tens of thousands of dollars.

Q. Should I buy modern Platinum and Gold Eagles for their rarity?

A. Absolutely not! The modern platinum and Gold Eagles are nothing more than our government's bullion coin, similar to the Krugerrand, the Maple Leaf, the Chinese Panda, and the Mexican Onza. It's the exact same thing. Some dealers will say, "This year they only made 34,000 half-ounce coins and that year they made a 100,000 of them, so obviously, the 34,000 are going to become a rare coin." That is a very "created" market. It's a way that dealers can buy bullion coins and still make their horrendous fifty to a hundred percent markup.

You don't have to believe me. All you have to do is look at the history of the last modern bullion coins sold as "rare." The trend started in 1982 with the Chinese Pandas. China made new modern bullion coins. They made up to a twelve-ounce gold piece. For about four years, they were the hottest things in the market. Was there money to be made? Yes, if you were a speculator and you bought them immediately when they came out, sold them immediately if they went up, and you didn't hold them. It was pure speculation, pure gambling, and a lot of people made a lot of money. A lot of people lost a lot of money, too. But now, twenty years later, I doubt if there's one in a thousand of those bullion coins that were made in China, England, or Australia that have more than a five or 10 % premium over their melt value. Today, some dealers are trying the same thing that failed twenty years ago. I don't see that trend changing. It's a losing proposition.

Q. What should I expect to pay for half-ounce gold and half-ounce platinum coins?

A. What you're going to find is that the premium will vary depending on how backlogged the government is and who's promoting the coins. In general, to buy half-ounce platinum or half-ounce gold, you should expect to pay anywhere from 9 % over spot (spot is the going price that day of gold or platinum) to possibly 15% over spot.

Q. Should I buy gold bullion, silver, or platinum?

A. In my opinion, bullion is by far the safest most liquid way to hedge your money or invest in an alternative to paper. It is insurance against economic catastrophe. I believe investing in these metals makes more sense than rare coins for most people.

If it turns out that the predictions are wrong, it can be sold later for a small loss or gain as the market dictates at that time. I don't recommend putting all your money into gold or silver as a way to get rich quick. Physical bullion is normally bought as a hedge for a perceived crisis or as "feel good" insurance. Although the last ten years have been phenomenal, they will rarely serve as an actual moneymaking investment unless you just happen to get lucky with timing.

People have made significant money buying and holding gold or silver. Many have not made money since 1979, primarily because they were talked into coins like $20 St. Gaudens and Liberties or silver dollars, which will probably result in a large loss. See chapter 10 on bullion for a more detailed look at platinum, gold, and silver.

Q. I've been told that coins are private and don't have to be reported to the government for taxes or tariffs.

A. This is partially true. As a coin dealer, if you sell me coins or semi-rare coins, or even many of the bullion coins, I do not report it to the IRS or any other government agency. However, if you make money on the coins, you're obligated to report it on your income tax. So, I guess it's really two different questions: (1) Can you get away with not reporting it? Or, (2) Are you supposed to report it?

Anyone who's telling you they're private and nothing has to be reported so you can pass them on to your kids without going through your estate is basically telling you to break the law.

Buried in the new health care bill, which passed in 2010, is a new law that will require all transactions over $600 to be reported on a 1099. This is scheduled to start in 2012, and President Obama has started hiring 18,000 new IRS agents to deal with it.

Q. In taking such a large loss, should I just leave these coins to my grandkids? Maybe they'll be worth something in fifty years.

A. I'm a big fan of keeping things simple. If you want to leave something to your heirs, why not make it a basic, easy investment. Cash is always good. If you want to leave gold, you should trade your rare coins for bullion coins such as Eagles. Why are you going to give a mistake to someone who knows little about it?

I hear excuses all the time about this. I know the heirs are getting something for free, but the reality is the real reason people do this sometimes is that they just don't want to face the truth. They want it buried along with them.

Recently, I had to settle an estate. It's not fun to go through someone else's mess. It's time consuming. It's a hassle, and it's frustrating to deal with on top of everything else that goes on when someone dies.

I advise against ignoring a large loss. In many cases, people held these coins fifteen to twenty years, and they're only worth half of what they spent on them. In my opinion, fifteen to twenty years is a long-term investment. It's an investment that just hasn't paid off. They miss out on favorable tax consequences.

We buy a lot of coins from people who do inherit them or get them as presents. What you're going to stick your heirs with is your problem. If you don't want to deal with it, you're just passing it along to people who, nine out of ten times, know even less than you do. Either they sell them for half of what they're worth, or they stick them in a closet, and they're so overwhelmed nothing ever happens to them.

When I see clients, I often hear, "My father left me these coins. I can't believe it." It's usually not a fond memory. I have bought, appraised, and attempted to explain rare coin portfolios to heirs literally hundreds of times. Most often, it's confusing and overwhelming unless its simple gold bullion coins or silver bullion–

type material. I've met people who have spent years trying to figure out what they had.

One group of four siblings inherited four hundred $20 St. Gaudens. It seemed a simple thing to split them up. Three of them wanted to keep the coins, and one wanted to sell. So, why not each take one hundred coins and be done with it?

The coins were not professionally graded, so they felt one person might get better coins than the rest. They didn't want to spend the money to certify them (about $20 per coin), so they tried to get a dealer to do an appraisal and separate the coins. However, most dealers are not that anxious to perform this task without a decent chance to buy the coins. Consequently, the dealers wanted to charge for the appraisal. Some of the heirs simply refused to pay for this service, so they continued to do nothing. The coins remained in a safe deposit box, earning no interest, only dust. In the meantime, no one has access to the coins or inheritance. Another woman who inherited a sizeable collection tried and tried to make sense of the coins. She looked for and found mounds of receipts and tried to match them to coins. Since she knew very little, she tried to get appraisals based on the receipts she had. Finally, she ended up with what she considered a conservative appraisal, which she used for estate tax purposes. Years later, we finally got together, and I purchased the coins.

Do your heirs a favor: deal with it while you are alive.

Q. Are there any hidden profits that I'm overlooking here?

A. Many people—and as painful, frustrating, and disappointing as it is to realize—find that there is some benefit in using the loss for tax purposes.

I'm not an accountant, so check with yours, but it is my understanding that you can take a capital loss on your coins similar to the way you would on stocks. You can then offset any capital gains against your capital losses. So, if you have gains, if you sold a house, sold real estate, or sold stocks for a profit or plan to in the future, you don't need to wait until you have a gain to take the loss, because the loss can carry forward indefinitely. It's a great time to take your loss on coins, because that absolutely puts money in your pocket.

The second thing you can do if you do not have capital gains is deduct $3,000 a year from your income (although there is talk of raising this to $8,250). Granted, if you lost $100,000, that might not add up fast enough. But that's $1,000 to $1,500 in your pocket every year, and what's wrong with an extra $1,000 a year? Again, these rules may change, so check with your own accountant.

Here's the ironic part. The people who don't sell because they have such a big loss pass it to their children or grandchildren. They pass coins through their estate, and whoever inherits those coins, inherits them at the lower value.

So, if you spent $100,000 and you don't want to take your loss because those coins are only worth $30,000 today, you now pass those coins on through inheritance to your grandchildren. Your grandchildren now get those coins at $30,000 value! Let's suppose, by some miracle, you're right, and five years after you die those coins take off. Those coins go back to $100,000 somehow. Now, the people who inherited those coins are paying taxes on the $70,000 "gain." You didn't get the loss, and they get to pay the tax because the coins' value went back to what you paid. It costs your heirs as much as $30,000 in taxes for you to finally break even.

Q. My dealer says if I complete a set of coins, for example a set of $2½ Indians, Walking Liberties or an eight-piece gold set or Roll set of Franklin Halves they automatically go up in value by 30 %.

A. This is a complete lie.
This is a long-held myth that has been promoted by dealers for obvious reasons. They'd rather sell you a group of coins rather than one coin. It's in their interest to sell a set. If you really can make 30

% by simply putting sets together, I, as a dealer, would be doing nothing more than accumulating coins, putting sets together, and selling them back into the market. I could be putting sets together all day long and making 30 % on them without dealing with clients, talking to anyone, and without the paperwork and expense of running a business. If that were true, why would a dealer be telling you this? Everyone would be doing that. Look at any of the major auctions. Look at the trend in the last twenty to thirty years. A lot of the major auctions include complete sets of gold or complete sets of proof coins or sets that you absolutely could not reassemble. So, you're talking about a one-of-a-kind type of set. If any set should have a premium, it should be something you couldn't reproduce. In almost every case, the auctioneer gets the most money for that set by breaking it apart and selling it coin by coin.

I handled the finest know registry set of of $10 Indians and three of the finest $2½ Indians and had to sell the sets as individual coins to maximize the price. Most dealers will do the same. When selling, I have to get top dollar for my clients, and the labor, sweat, and tears that go into assembling the sets have little market value.

It is very rare that a set brings more than the sum. In fact, it usually brings less.

Q. My dealer said if I complete a particular set he could sell it next year to a collector in Europe who's buying these.

A. First of all, the best market you're going to have for U.S. coins is right here in the United States. Again, there's always the rare exception, but beware if someone is promising you that next year they have a buyer in Europe or Japan or somewhere else who's going to buy it and double your money. I think you have to do one of two things:

1. Realize it for the scam it is, or

2. Tell them you'd like it in writing.

One client I met spent $500,000 on rare California Fractional Gold pieces. These were privately made gold coins of 25c, 50c, and $1. They are fairly rare, historically fun, but thinly traded with few price references.

He was told to complete a set and hold them for a year. At that time, the plan was to auction them in England for $1.25 million. Truly an unbelievable story once he thought about it. The time to sell drew near, and suddenly his phone calls and letters went unanswered. He contacted the New York attorney general for help. They wrote letters and made calls and found the company had disappeared, the phone disconnected, and the principals nowhere to be found.

He was stuck with coins he knew nothing about. I was able to get the coins valued for him. After another month of dead ends pursuing the company, he finally sold for $34,350. His parting comment as I packed up his coins and walked out of his kitchen was that his kids wouldn't get an inheritance now.

Q. I never lose money on investments, so I can't take a loss on these coins.

A. If this is true, you're probably the only person I ever met who's never lost on anything. I don't care how good an investor you are, everyone I know has lost money on something—it's part of learning how to invest. So, it either means anything you didn't make money on you're still sitting with because you haven't sold it, or you've been very, very lucky.

There's no shame in selling at a loss. And, if it's actually true that this is your first loss, I mean, if you have actually never lost money, that means you have a lot of capital gains. You should take the loss and offset your gains.

Q. I'm really worried about the economy and the world situation. Shouldn't I own rare coins?

A. Absolutely not. I love coins, but they do not protect you against inflation, a falling dollar, or global unrest. If you were really concerned, I'd buy some gold bullion or bullion coins. By that, I mean Krugerrands, Maple Leafs, one-ounce bars, American Eagles, or silver. Or investigate gold or mining stocks or ETFs, if you're trying to make money and not just hedge.

If the dollar drops against other currencies, the likelihood of your gold and silver going up is very good. Rare coins are not affected by the dollar, inflation, or political unrest. I'd consider platinum in that mix, along with gold. But if you're completely wrong and the economy booms for ten years, platinum tends to go up when the economy booms because of the industrial use. It's a nice hedge. For more information on gold, silver, and platinum, see chapter 10.

Q. I've been told there's a huge silver deficit and we'll soon run out of silver and the price will skyrocket.

A. The only reason I'd tell you to buy silver is to have a hedge or speculation. In other words, if you're really afraid of what's happening in this country and you're really afraid of the government, you buy a bag of silver dimes, quarters, and halves and throw it under your bed for that worst-case scenario. You do not buy silver to get rich. The Hunt Brothers tried it in 1979 and lost a fortune. They were not dumb guys. They were billionaires, and they managed to lose almost everything they had by thinking the same thing about silver. There are reports out there by people who are self-proclaimed experts.

What you have to remember is silver, unlike gold, is actually consumed. It's industrial. My point here is, the same people who are touting huge silver profits have been saying that on and off for the last twenty years, and strongly for the last six. In fact, one article written six years ago said, "We can't possibly have enough silver to last us another two years." That means, we should have run out of silver four years ago. Today silver is still very cheap. What that tells you is their supply number must be wrong. They're saying, "We only have 'so much' and we're using up 'x' amount." I believe we're probably using up "x" amount, but all this proves to me is that the number they quote when they say we only have "so much" is obviously wrong if we still have cheap silver. Right?

I constantly get calls from brokers telling me silver is going up, and I need to buy it from them right now. The first thing I would tell you is never buy spur of the moment. I don't care if it's silver, gold, platinum, or coins. It's rare that waiting overnight or hanging up and thinking about it for an hour is going to change the price. If you want to buy silver, or if you want to buy anything, I would recommend that you call one or two or three other dealers and ask them for a price on the same thing. Silver, gold, and platinum are much easier to price than rare coins, because we don't care what it looks like. Silver is silver. Gold is gold. A Maple Leaf's a Maple Leaf. A bag of silver is a bag of silver. So, you have no quality assurance to worry about, which you might have with other coins. So, at least hang up and call two or three dealers and see if you're being offered a fair price. My experience has been when dealers or brokers are trying to force you to make a purchase right there, that minute on the phone, they're charging you too much. I know there are at least one or two dealers who are marking up silver 30 to 40 % percent. That's like buying stocks and paying your stockbroker a 30 or 40 % commission on stock. It's like going to the bank and telling them you want to break a hundred dollar bill and getting seventy dollars back. You'd never do that. So, never do it with silver or gold. Silver and gold are money.

Q. After reading your book, I don't think there are any good dealers out there. Is that true?

A. That's absolutely false. There are hundreds of good dealers out there. The problem is they're just not necessarily the guys calling you on the phone every week, trying to sell you coins.

We've given you plenty of ways to check out the dealers. Check out their references. Check out the organization they belong to. The intent is not to bash the industry or dealers; it is simply to educate investors and show them how to avoid pitfalls and pay the right prices from the right dealers. This is the only way to strengthen the coin market.

I want you to separate yourself as an investor or collector. I also talk about promoters. I frequently have different opinions about investing in certain items. The promoters and specialists certainly create and move markets. They create excitement and share their knowledge with new collectors. They also provide opportunity for investors to take profits.

And while I do bash certain practices—because I see the novice investor's losses afterward—I should tell you the bulk of the dealers are good, honest, well-meaning people.

I have nothing but admiration for the dealers who founded PCGS and later NGC. These dealers did more to further knowledge to collectors and investors than any other group in numismatic history. Because of PCGS and NGC, there is more readily available information than ever, information dealers would've paid tens of thousands of dollars for before 1986. You, as an investor, simply need to use it.

This all being said, many dealers feel I'm bad for the industry because I don't advocate coins for every investor. This book is more for the novice or casual investor than the seasoned, active investor/collector who reads all the available publications, including *Coin Dealer Newsletter*, *Coin World*, and *Numismatic News*. This book is aimed more at those who bought as a hedge and/or investment, sometimes from brokers over the phone who were simply trying to make commission. People who bought without the benefit of being true collectors or having anything but a vague idea about rare coins.

Q. How can I make money in coins?

A. There are three ways, as discussed earlier in the book:

1. Learn the market. Invest the time. Invest the effort and pick a lot of minds.

2. Find one of those relatively few dealers who have a proven program of following their client's coins and profiting. I'm not sure anyone has really made much the last eleven years.

3. Stay out of them! This won't make you money, but it could keep you from losing, which is just as good. My company trades tens of millions of dollars worth of coins every year. But even with that, we have clients who have lost money. So there's never a guarantee. You've got to go in with that in mind, and if you can't or won't, you shouldn't be in this market—pure and simple.

Bullion has far out-performed most rare coins by a huge margin.

Q. I bought coins years ago, and they're not worth what I paid for them. But I can't afford to take the loss.

A. Minimize your loss. I feel that unless you have something really spectacular, you take the loss and you move on. Sitting on something that has little chance of appreciating and just hoping is not going to make the loss go away. So, unless you have real concrete reasons why your material's going to go back up, take the loss.

We see people every day who have had that same "hold and hope" philosophy for fifteen to twenty years and have lost 70 to 90 % of their value. That's the average. Other people we see have been in it for three or four years, and they're losing 30 to 50 %. So again, if you just look at the numbers, in three or four years, would you rather lose 50 %, or would you rather drag it out to fifteen years so you'll lose 90 %?

If you believe rare coins are going up, it follows that you must believe gold and silver are also going up. Switch into easily traded bullion coins, and you have a much better chance of making up your losses. One client took a $170,000 loss in 1999 on my recommendation. We put the money into gold bullion coins. Not only did he make up his loss, he is now ahead by $370,000.

Q. What do you have to report to the government?

A. There are only a few different things that the government requires. Basic reporting includes certain gold coins, like gold bars, kilo bars, Krugerrands, or Maple Leafs.

Also reportable is a bag of silver, a thousand ounces of silver, and if you, as a client, spend $10,000 or more in cash per year.

It is incumbent on you, and it's expected for you to take the appropriate legal stance of reporting gains, losses, and income. See your accountant for details, as these requirements change from time to time.

This is set to change in 2012, when the new law will require anything sold for more than $600 to be reported. No exception for rare coins.

Q. I want to trade my coins. One company is offering me 30 % more for my coins than anyone else is offering me. But they want me to trade. Should I do that? Am I getting a good deal?

A. I think this type of trade is very similar to a car dealer. If you're trading, he's going to make money on one side or the other.

The fact is that most dealers get their pricing from the same sources. Believe it or not, the top fifteen to twenty-five dealers run the market.

Why is a dealer going to pay you more than what he could pay simply by picking up the phone and buying from another dealer.

Make sure you get an offer in writing. Not an indication, a real offer. Many dealers won't do this. Until you get it, you don't have a deal.

Some dealers will claim their coins are worth more than market but then do everything they can to convince you not to sell, or they simply trade you into more coins in which they can hide the true price.

Others tell you they are worth more simply to save face, keep you from going elsewhere, or so that they don't reveal their true markup.

One high-profile dealer is selling Swiss 20 franc coins for about $395 and claiming a 30 to 35 % markup. This would mean they are paying about $300 for them. Yet, simply finding prices on the Internet shows other dealers selling the same coin for as little as $244!

Q. Shouldn't I just wait if I have to sell my coins at a loss? After all, I'll only get one, two or three percent if I put my money in a safe CD.

A. My response is two or three percent is better than a negative return. You are not protecting your money by being illiquid and in a market that, overall, has only moved twenty-nine percent in eleven years.

Q. Why are you the only dealer telling me to stay out of rare coins?

A. I love rare coins. I believe for some people they can be a great addition to a portfolio. What I have a problem with is a dealer who tries to sell overpriced coins, whether they're common or rare coins, as investments. And they never tell you when to sell or even offer to help you sell. Unfortunately, the majority of brokers and telemarketers are charging such high prices you're practically guaranteed to lose money. My problem is not with coins; it's with the scoundrels out there who are telling you to cash in your IRAs and pay the taxes, pay the penalties, and on top of that, pay them half of that in commissions. We run into brokers and dealers who are telling people to take home equity loans to buy coins. That's where I have my problem.

Most brokers care only about their commissions.

Q. I want to exchange my coins for gold. How should I do this?

A. Get a cash offer first. Then, check the price of the bullion you are trading into. Make sure that prices are realistic so that your money is not disappearing in the trade. As a courtesy and a service to clients, some dealers will liquidate coins for you and arrange for you to purchase or convert your proceeds to bullion.

If you trade, our practice is to sell the bullion to you wholesale, which normally will give you an extra 3 % savings. It could be meaningful on a large transaction.

Q. I've noticed a lot of coins being offered on TV shopping networks. Are they good buys?

A. While it certainly is fun to see the different offerings and hear the history and explanations, these coins are usually expensive. If you are just having fun and getting caught up in the moment, that's fine. A lot of people do it, as is evidenced by the huge dollar volume these marketers do.

Realize you are paying a very high price for this convenience. I do not recommend anyone who is serious about collecting or investing to buy this way.

Q. My dealer says I'll get the most money by auctioning my coins. Is that the best way to go?

A. If you have a one-of-a-kind collection or the ultra rarities, it may be worth looking at auction. However, for some people, an auction can be the worst way to go. Some dealers recommend auctions so they don't have to repurchase coins or accept responsibility for the price.

The truth is many coins bring below average prices at auctions.

For more information, see chapter 24, 25, and 26.

Many point to occasional reports of record-breaking auction prices. That's because when an extremely rare coin breaks a record, it gets great press. Certainly, if you have those types of coins, an auction is worth considering.

More often, coins will barely bring wholesale. In fact, article after article in *Coin Dealer Newsletter* warns collectors about coins consistently selling for as much as 30 or 40 % less than bid at auction. Coin sales of 20 % to a whopping 72 % less than wholesale bid are well documented! Deduct commission from this, and you can see that the seller received only a fraction of the true value of the coins. *Coin Dealer Newsletter* further states, "The amount of money consignors are losing by not doing their homework just amazes us."

During a strong gold market and what many dealers are touting as a "heated-up" coin market, we find yet another disclaimer in *Certified Coin Dealer Newsletter*. While blatantly stating the coin market is, "off to the races" the *Certified Coin Dealer Newsletter* also states, "However, it is important to point out that discounting is also playing a healthy role. We usually see a fair amount of discounting when auctions are held and these past 10 days of auctions provided a vast amount of needed material. The coins that were offered with no or low reserves were certainly vulnerable to discounting. Consequently it is not unusual to see declines, sometimes even severe drops."

Q. My dealer is saying that you tell people to sell so you can buy coins for yourself. And it's not in clients' best interest.

A. Selling coins to investors is easier than buying coins from them, because usually I am the bearer of bad news. This type of claim is ridiculous. Any dealer is making a markup, markdown, or commission whether they buy or sell. When I, for example, buy coins from collectors/investors, I pay a percentage less than I know I will resell the coins for. Typically, the coins are resold within days or weeks of the purchase. It is rare for any dealer who purchases coins from collectors/investors to hold them for any length of time. Certainly, it's silly to believe that a dealer would buy this way for his own account.

Most purchase for their own collections from other dealers or at shows. After all, that way they can choose coins before they ever get to the investors or collectors.

The flip side is this: why is this dealer selling to you if he believes coins are going up? Using his logic, it would be in his interest to hold coins if he believed what he said. Maybe he is simply "unloading" unwanted coins and not really helping his clients.

The fact is many dealers have different opinions. That's what makes the market function. However, I guarantee you that the overwhelming majority of clients who sold coins over the past sixteen years are far better off than those who bought from most dealers. I would guess as high as 95 % of these buyers have lost 30 % or more!

Q. I bought from a dealer with the same religious convictions as I. Don't you think this safeguards me?

A. We all like to do business with people with whom we have something in common. It's simply human nature.

However, just because you both believe in the same religion, politics, and so on, does nothing to guarantee this person knows anything about coins. Just turn on the TV and see how many paid spokesmen are pushing rare coins. One doesn't even know the coin jargon and calls them "antique coins." No one with even a tiny bit of coin knowledge uses that term. So how much more do you think he really knows about coins?

Bill O'Reilly was on television saying that even though he had coin dealers advertise on his show, it was the viewer's responsibility to do his own due diligence.

A spokesperson, clergy member, or someone with same beliefs may be the most honest person in the world, but without intimate knowledge of the market, he may not be able to help you make money.

Beware of people falsely telling you what you want to hear to get your money. Unfortunately, there are a lot of them around. It's your money. It is your obligation to check out the dealer's reputation, prices, markups, and so on, just as you would anyone else's. Just because a dealer claims to be religious or advertises in religious or political media doesn't mean they are the best at helping you make money.

APPENDIX

RECOMMENDED READING

Robert Prechter, *Conquer the Crash*, available at most bookstores, Amazon, and at *www.elliottwave.com/conquer*

Coin Dealer Newsletter, P.O. Box 11099, Torrance, CA 90510

Certified Coin Dealer Newsletter, PO Box 7939, Torrance, CA 90504-9339

ANA *Grading Standards*, available at most bookstores

R. S. Yeoman, *The Official Red Book: A Guide Book of United States Coins*

R. S. Yeoman, *The Official Blue Book Handbook of United States Coins*

IMPORTANT ORGANIZATIONS

Professional Numismatic Guild (PNG)
3950 Concordia Lane
Fallbrook, CA 92028
(760) 728-1300

American Numismatic Association (ANA)
818 N. Cascade Avenue
Colorado Springs, CO 80903-3379
(719) 633-2646

Professional Coin Grading Service (PCGS)
P.O. Box 9458
New Port Beach, CA 92658
(800) 447-8848

Numismatic Guaranty Corp (NGC)
P.O. Box 4776
Sarasota, FL 34230
(941) 360-3990

GLOSSARY

ANA—American Numismatic Association, 818 N. Cascade Avenue, Colorado Springs, Colorado, 80903-3379, 719-633-2646:

This is the largest organization dedicated to coin collectors in the country and is a great source of information and fun for collectors. They also have a grading service called ANACS, which provides an unbiased opinion of quality. They do not provide any guarantees of accuracy, as do PCGS or NGC.

CERTIFIED COINS:
Generally, these are coins graded by independent grading companies NGC and PCGS.

GRADING SYSTEM:
This is the way the quality of coins is denoted. The system is a combination of words and numbers, from Poor to Uncirculated and 0 to 70.

Grading Abbreviations

Corresponding numbers may be used with any of these descriptions.

- MS-70 Perfect Uncirculated
- MS-67 Gem Uncirculated
- MS-65 Choice Uncirculated
- MS-63 Select Uncirculated
- MS-60 Uncirculated
- AU-55 Choice About Uncirculated
- AU-50 About Uncirculated
- EF-45 Choice Extremely Fine
- EF-40 Extremely Fine
- VF-30 Choice Very Fine
- VF-20 Very Fine
- F-12 Fine
- VG-8 Very Good
- G-4 Good
- AG-3 About Good

Circulated coins range from 0 to 58. Uncirculated range from MS (mint state-)-60 to MS-70, with MS-70 being absolutely perfect. PR, or proof coins, are typically PR 60–PR 70, although mishandled proofs can be graded lower.

GREY SHEET:

This term is actually what dealers call the Coin Dealer Newsletter (CDN). The CDN is the absolute best representation of coin values in the country. The main publication is published weekly. There is also a monthly and quarterly publication for coins that trade a bit more infrequently. In addition, they publish the Certified Coin Dealer Newsletter for PCGS, IGC, and a variety of other services. The people who assemble prices for the CDN painstakingly watch transactions on teletype, CQS (the computerized wholesale trading network), auctions, and coin shows. While prices are not always one hundred percent to the penny, it is without question, the best information available. Proof of that is the fact that no credible dealer would dream of buying or selling without it! Go to a coin show, and you'll hear over and over again, "What's Grey Sheet on that coin?"

INDICATIONS:

A dealer will often send a sheet of what you assume to be "bids" but on further inspection, they will be referred to as Indications. This means this is what the dealer might think the coins were worth on the day, hour, or minute he looked them up. This will change with market conditions, inventory, dealer needs, or the fact that you actually want to sell the coins. They are not bids. Sometimes, these figures are what the dealer sells coins for or are based on if he really wants the coins. Do not depend on these figures if your intent is to sell.

NGC—Numismatic Grading Corp., P.O. Box 4776, Sarasota, FL 34230, 941-360-3990:

Like PCGS, NGC is highly regarded in the industry. Highly recommended. Their coins are easily traded and provide a high degree of liquidity.

PCGS—Professional Coin Grading Service, P.O. Box 9458, New Port Beach, CA 92658, 800-447-8848:
This was the first major grading company accepted by coin dealers and collectors, as well as the first to guarantee its grading. Started in 1986, it has become the largest grading company in the United States. We highly recommend PCGS. Their coins usually trade sight-unseen through a network of approximately a thousand dealers. The dealers who started PCGS and NGC have done more for the coin collector/investor than anyone in the industry. They made it possible for novices to buy properly graded coins and provided true guarantees on the coins they graded.

PNG—Professional Numismatic Guild, 3950 Concordia Lane, Fallbrook, CA 92028, 760-728-1300:
This is the most prestigious coin organization your dealer can belong to. All members must be screened and voted on. All members must adhere to a "Code of Ethics."
Being a member of PNG is perhaps one of the best credentials your dealer can have.

PREMIUMS:
Most bullion or semi-numismatic coins sell for more than the actual value of the gold or silver in them. The difference between the actual value of the precious metal and the value of the coin is the premium. For example, if spot gold is $1,500 and a Gold Eagle sells for $1,625, the premium is $125, or just over 8 %.

RAW COINS:
These are non-certified coins. Any coins not graded by companies like PCGS and, NGC and are considered "raw" by dealers. These are coins graded by the dealer who sold them or by an unrecognized grading company.

SPREAD:
The difference between the buy and sell price is the spread. For example, the wholesale spread on Gold Eagles can typically be $12 over spot bid and $15 over spot ask. This is a $3 spread.

One dealer on the Internet discloses a 30 % spread and explains that this means he sells for $500 and purchases for 30 % less, or $350. The spread is exclusive of commission. So, on top of this spread could be a dealer or broker commission or markup.

SPOT:
Spot price is the base price for gold, silver, platinum, and so on. The actual price of a bullion coin will be based on spot price. There will usually be a slightly higher price than spot on a coin or bar when you purchase.

VALUE:
This seemingly simple word needs definition as used in this book. If you don't believe it, call your dealer for the "value" of your coins. Often, they will qualify that by asking, "Do you mean if you are buying or selling?"

Value is the price a coin trades at before commissions. It is the price that I, as a dealer can either buy or sell a coin. For example, on a common coin such as a $20 St. Gaudens in MS-63, I might be able to go into the market and find sellers at the same price as buyers. My profit would be a commission or markup/markdown.

It's similar to a stock. When you see on TV that ABC stock closed at $70, it means the last trade was $70 per share. Of course the stockbroker charges a commission, or fee, on that $70. So the stock is both bought and sold at $70—the value. Therefore, as an investor, you need to know not only the value but what you will net if you sell, or what your actual price is when you buy. Price and value are not necessarily the same.

ADDED BONUS

Throughout the book, I recommend getting current valuations. I also talk about the thousand charts I made to do Performance Reviews. These reviews are a unique feature that is ONLY offered by American Federal. Using these Reviews we can show you how almost any coin you own or are contemplating has done in relation to each other, as well as gold or silver. For example, if you are thinking of buying $20 St. Gaudens in MS-63 or MS-66, I can print a chart to see which is the best performer. In this case, I see that MS-63s went up 200 % since 1999, while MS-66 only went up 57 %. This, of course, does not guarantee that the MS-63 will be the better coin in the future, but it certainly gives you valuable information for your decision.

Since you took the time to read this book, I am offering this specialized information to you as a bonus. No one else I know of has or is willing to share this kind if data with you. More likely, they want to provide information only on the coin they are trying to sell you.

American Federal has always offered a no-obligation appraisal. This offer is for a verbal valuation. We really do check auction records, past prices from other dealers, and a history of what we have handled here at American Federal over the past thirty years. Our system lets us look up what we were able to buy and sell coins for in the market. It allows us to find the person looking for certain coins. We keep track of both collectors and dealers serving them.

Sometimes, we have to do extensive research. For example, I purchased a major Territorial collection that was quite difficult to price out, because it is a very specialized and small esoteric market.

I have purchased some of the finest know Registry sets of certified coins, including the top $10 Indian set, several top $2½ Indian sets, as well as single rarities that sold for hundreds of thousand of dollars each.

On the following pages are convenient sheets you can use for both of the Reviews we offer. Simply fill them out and fax (480) 553-5290, mail, or e-mail *info@americanfederal.com*. Call 800-221-7694 with questions.

AMERICAN FEDERAL RARE COIN & BULLION

P.O. Box 5810 • Carefree, AZ 85377
Phone (800) 221-7694 • Fax (480) 553-5290

FREE OFFER

DETACH COMPLETED FREE OFFER FORM ALONG DOTTED LINE

CONFIDENTIAL PORTFOLIO ESTIMATE SHEET

Immediate Evaluation Required

Qty of Coin(s)	Date on Coin	Mint Mark	Grading Service	Grade of Coin	Description of Coin
			EXAMPLE		
2	1924	none	PCGS	MS63	$20 St Gaudens

For longer coin lists copy this form or use the additional forms enclosed

B-01

AMERICAN FEDERAL RARE COIN & BULLION

P.O. Box 5810 • Carefree, AZ 85377

Phone (800) 221-7694 • Fax (480) 553-5290

FREE OFFER

CONFIDENTIAL PORTFOLIO ESTIMATE SHEET

Immediate Evaluation Required

Qty of Coin(s)	Date on Coin	Mint Mark	Grading Service	Grade of Coin	Description of Coin
			EXAMPLE		
2	1924	none	PCGS	MS63	$20 St Gaudens

For longer coin lists copy this form or use the additional forms enclosed

B-01

DETACH COMPLETED FREE OFFER FORM ALONG DOTTED LINE